WE ARE
NOT YET
EQUAL

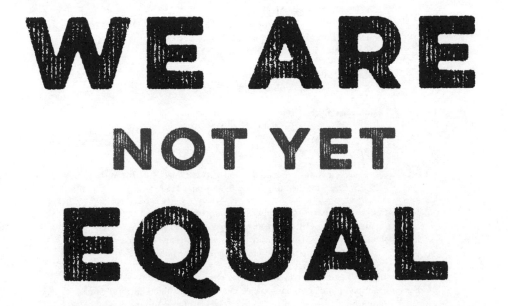

WE ARE
NOT YET
EQUAL

UNDERSTANDING OUR RACIAL DIVIDE

CAROL ANDERSON

WITH
TONYA BOLDEN

BLOOMSBURY

NEW YORK LONDON OXFORD NEW DELHI SYDNEY

BLOOMSBURY YA
Bloomsbury Publishing Inc., part of Bloomsbury Publishing Plc
1385 Broadway, New York, NY 10018

BLOOMSBURY and the Diana logo are trademarks of
Bloomsbury Publishing Plc

First published in the United States of America in September 2018
by Bloomsbury YA

Bloomsbury books may be purchased for business or promotional use.
For information on bulk purchases please contact Macmillan Corporate and
Premium Sales Department at specialmarkets@macmillan.com

Library of Congress Cataloging-in-Publication Data
Names: Anderson, Carol (Carol Elaine), author.
Title: We are not yet equal : understanding our racial divide / by Carol Anderson.
Other titles: Understanding our racial divide
Description: New York : Bloomsbury, [2018]
Identifiers: LCCN 2018024234 (print) | LCCN 2018025921 (e-book)
ISBN 978-1-5476-0076-2 (hardcover) • ISBN 978-1-5476-0078-6 (e-book)
Subjects: LCSH: African Americans—Civil rights—History—Juvenile literature. |
African Americans—Politics and government—Juvenile literature. |
African Americans—Social conditions—Juvenile literature. | Whites—United States—
Attitudes—History—Juvenile literature. | Whites—United States—Politics and government—
Juvenile literature. | Opposition (Political science)—United States—History—Juvenile
literature. | Racism—United States—History—Juvenile literature. | United States—Race
relations—History—Juvenile literature.
Classification: LCC E185.61.A5437 2018 (print) | LCC E185.61 (e-book) |
DDC 323.1196/073—dc23
LC record available at https://lccn.loc.gov/2018024234

Book design by Vikki Sheatsley
Typeset by Westchester Publishing Services
Printed and bound in the U.S.A. by Berryville Graphics Inc., Berryville, Virginia
2 4 6 8 10 9 7 5 3 1

All papers used by Bloomsbury Publishing Plc are natural, recyclable products
made from wood grown in well-managed forests. The manufacturing processes
conform to the environmental regulations of the country of origin.

To find out more about our authors and books visit www.bloomsbury.com
and sign up for our newsletters.

To those who aspired and paid the price
—C. A.

For lovers of history, seekers of truth
—T. B.

CONTENTS

FOREWORD

My high school US History teacher, Mr. Tripathi, was Indian American. In fact, if I remember correctly, he and I were the only two people in the classroom—out of twenty-five or so—with brown skin.

But that's not something we ever talked about. In fact, it took until now, fifteen years later, for me to recognize how remarkable it was that *he* was the teacher. That fifty years after the first African Americans stepped into a previously segregated school in the South, an Indian immigrant was teaching US History in one of the most racially *and* socioeconomically diverse high schools in the state of Georgia. Clearly change *was* possible.

In 1960, one of those first students, six-year-old Ruby Bridges, was escorted into the William Frantz Elementary School in New Orleans by her mother and four federal US Marshals; she spent her entire first day in the principal's office. Like Ruby, I was the only black kid in that US History class. Honestly, I was the only black kid in *most* of my high school classes. Despite Norcross High's diversity, courses were stratified into three levels: college prep, honors, and gifted-honors/AP/IB. The higher up the "class-level" pyramid you climbed, the whiter—and richer—the class-rooms became. I was the token at that gifted honors level.

But back then, it would've been "in poor taste" to point it out.

Which is why I think Mr. Tripathi never acknowledged his ethnicity, despite the fact that it could've been used as an example of just how far we'd come as a nation. Back then, "colorblindness" was the name of the game. Acknowledging that the only other spot of brown in the US History classroom was the teacher—and how problematic that was—would've been considered *divisive*. It'd been a long time since Dr. King and his contemporaries did away with Jim Crow during the Civil Rights Movement, and "progress" meant we were all the same. Racism was no longer a thing.

Except now we know that's not—and has never been—true. Now, statistics show undeniable discrepancies in arrest and incar-ceration rates along racial lines. Now, unarmed black men and women are gunned down in the streets for nothing more than looking "suspicious." Now, people openly gather in the name of "white nationalism" and raise the Nazi salute as they rally around discriminatory and xenophobic ideas.

Now it *can't* be denied that racism in America is still very much a thing.

But why? Why are we *still* here? What paradigms perpetuate racism in our society? What seemingly innocent—if not *patriotic*—ideas are actually racist in origin?

And what do we do about it? What do we *say*? Racism is a

topic so fraught, so taboo these days, the very mention of it causes instant discomfort for most people. How do we discuss both the origins of American racism and its manifestations—past and present—in a way that leads to mutual understanding and a desire for change? Is that even possible?

I think it is.

And I think this book, this journey from the end of American chattel slavery through the twentieth century and into the present day—exposing the roots of American racism, as well as the branches, boughs, and still-sprouting leaves—is an excellent place to start.

—*Nic Stone*

PROLOGUE

KINDLING

The seed for this book began to germinate many years ago, in the aftermath of a black man's death at the hands of the police: that of Amadou Diallo, a twenty-two-year-old West African immigrant. Diallo was mowed down in a hail of New York Police Department (NYPD) bullets on February 4, 1999, as he stood in the vestibule of his apartment building in the Soundview section of the Bronx, New York.

Though the killing was horrific enough—the police fired forty-one bullets, nineteen of which hit their target—what was truly stunning was the policy rationale espoused by New York City mayor Rudy Giuliani. On the news show *Nightline*, the mayor, virtually ignoring Diallo's death, glibly spouted one statistic after the next to demonstrate how the NYPD was the "most restrained and best behaved police department you could imagine."

Mayor Giuliani touted policies that had reduced crime in

New York City, and dismissed black peoples' concerns about racial profiling, stop and frisk, and police brutality. If those poorer neighborhoods that happened to be primarily black did not have this increased police activity, he asserted, the police would be accused of caring only about the affluent. Giuliani then countered that the real issue was the "community's racism against the police" and unwillingness to take responsibility for the issues plaguing their neighborhoods.

But restrained and behaved police don't fire forty-one bullets at an unarmed man. Moreover, New York's aggressive law enforcement policy appeared to expend most of its energy on the groups bringing the smallest yield of criminal activity. In 1999, blacks and Latinos, who made up 50 percent of New York City's population, accounted for 84 percent of those stopped and frisked by the NYPD, while the majority of illegal drugs and weapons were found on the relatively small number of whites detained by police.

There obviously was so much more going on here with Amadou Diallo's death than what was actually being discussed by the media, more than Giuliani was letting on, and more than even the most outraged discussions in the beauty shops and barbershops and churches and classrooms managed to pinpoint. Only I didn't know what to call it, what to name the unsettling and disturbing performance by Giuliani that I had just witnessed.

Fifteen years later, I experienced that same feeling, although the circumstances this time were somewhat different.

In August 2014, following the police shooting of eighteen-year-old Michael Brown, Ferguson, Missouri, went up in flames. Commentators throughout the print and digital media served up variations of the same story: black people, angered by the police killing of an unarmed black teen, were taking out their frustration in unproductive and predictable ways—rampaging, burning, and looting.

Framing the discussion—dominating it, in fact—was an overwhelming focus on black rage. Op-eds and news commentators debated whether Michael Brown was surrendering to or assaulting a police officer when six bullets took him down. They wrangled over whether Brown was really an innocent or a "thug" who had just committed a strong-arm robbery.

The question seemed to be whether black people were justified in their rage, even if that rage manifested itself in the most destructive, nonsensical ways. Again and again, across America's ideological spectrum, the issue was framed in terms of black rage, which, it seemed to me, entirely missed the point.

Epiphany.

What was really at work here was *white* rage. With so much attention focused on the flames, everyone had ignored the logs, the kindling. In some ways, it is easy to see why. White rage is not only about visible violence, but rather it works its way through the courts, the legislatures, and a range of government bureaucracies. It wreaks havoc subtly, almost imperceptibly. Too imperceptibly, certainly, for a nation consistently drawn to the spectacular— to what it can see. It's not just the Klan. White rage doesn't have to wear sheets, burn crosses, or take to the streets. Working the halls of power, it can achieve its ends far more effectively, far more destructively.

The trigger for white rage, inevitably, is black advancement. It is not the mere presence of black people that is the problem;

rather, it is blackness with ambition, with drive, with purpose, with aspirations, and with demands for full and equal citizenship. It is blackness that refuses to accept subjugation, to give up. A formidable array of policy assaults and legal contortions has consistently punished black resilience, black resolve.

And all the while, white rage manages to maintain not only the upper hand but also, apparently, the moral high ground. It's Giuliani chastising black people to fix the problems in their own neighborhoods instead of always scapegoating the police. It's the endless narratives about a culture of black poverty that devalues education, hard work, family, and ambition. It's a mantra told so often that some black people themselves have come to believe it. Few even think anymore to question the stories, the "studies" of black fathers abandoning their children, of rampant drug use in black neighborhoods, of black children hating education because doing well in school is "acting white"—all of which have been disproved.

In the wake of Ferguson I wrote an op-ed that ran in the *Washington Post*. In it, I set out to make white rage visible, to blow graphite onto that hidden fingerprint and trace its historic movements over the past 150 years, from the end of the Civil War and Reconstruction on down through the presidency of Barack Obama.

This book is an outgrowth of that op-ed. As I journey through Reconstruction, the Great Migration, *Brown v. Board of Education* and the rest of the Civil Rights Movement, and onward into the twenty-first century, it is my hope that you will see how white rage has undermined democracy; warped the Constitution; weakened the nation's ability to compete economically; squandered billions of dollars on baseless incarceration; rendered an entire region sick, poor, and woefully undereducated; and left cities nothing less than decimated. All this havoc has been wreaked simply because black people wanted to work, get an education, live in decent communities, raise their families, and vote. Because they were unwilling to take no for an answer.

It is only by recognizing the roots of this rage that we can build a future without it.

Crowds gather for Lincoln's second inauguration, in March 1865, shortly before the end of the Civil War.

"ORIGINAL SIN"

FOURTH US PRESIDENT AND FOUNDER JAMES Madison called America's engagement in the African slave trade the nation's "original sin."

The horrors of chattel slavery would bring down a wrath of biblical proportions, prophesied another founder, Thomas Jefferson, principal author of the Declaration of Independence. Like Madison, this third US president was a slaveholder.

"Indeed I tremble for my country when I reflect that God is just: that his justice cannot sleep forever," wrote Jefferson in the 1780s.

The day of reckoning came roughly eighty years later.

We now call it the Civil War.

This war erupted in mid-April 1861, when Confederate forces fired on the Union-held Fort Sumter in South Carolina's Charleston Harbor. Months earlier, in December 1860, South Carolina had seceded from the Union, then urged other slaveholding states to unite with it in creating a Confederate States of America (CSA). Eventually ten states did: Alabama, Arkansas, Florida, Georgia, Louisiana, North Carolina, Mississippi, Tennessee, Texas, and Virginia. (The slave states of Delaware, Kentucky, Maryland, and Missouri remained in the Union as did a slew of counties in western Virginia, the origins of the state of West Virginia in June 1863.)

The Confederacy's determination to establish "their independent slave republic," as historian James M. McPherson put it, led to four years of war, more than 1.5 million casualties, including perhaps as many as seven hundred and fifty thousand military deaths, along with an estimated fifty thousand civilian fatalities.

Added to this enormous loss of life, at war's end there were more than one million disabled ex-soldiers adrift. Countless widows sought help from a rickety veterans' pension system.

The mangled sinews of commerce in so much of the Southland only added to the despair.

Railroad tracks torn apart.

Fields fallow, hardened, and barren.

Bridges that once defied the physics of uncrossable rivers destroyed.

So many Southern cities had been reduced to smoldering rubble.

On March 4, 1865, in his second inaugural address, President Abraham Lincoln agonized that the war's carnage was God's punishment for "all the wealth piled by the bondsman's two hundred and fifty years of unrequited toil."

How would the nation atone?

That was the burning question for black people and progressive white people when the Confederacy began its surrender on April 9, 1865.

America was now at the crossroads between its slaveholding past and the possibility of a truly inclusive, vibrant democracy.

Would—could—the majority of white people come to see black people as equals?

In the process of rebuilding, of reconstructing the nation, would—could—political leaders have the clarity, humanity, and resolve to move the United States away from the racialized policies that had brought it to the edge of apocalypse?

Assigned to defend Washington, DC, twenty-seven soldiers of the 4th United States Colored Infantry pose in their Union uniforms. Nearly two hundred thousand black men and boys joined the Union army and navy, many with the hope that the end of the Civil War would bring black people full citizenship rights.

2

"BUT FOR YOUR RACE"

LONG BEFORE CANNON BOOM AND RIFLE SHOT ceased, President Abraham Lincoln made it clear that he would go easy on the rebels. This news was delivered in his Proclamation of Amnesty and Reconstruction, issued on December 8, 1863.

With some exceptions, including top Confederate leaders, if rebels swore allegiance to the Constitution and, essentially, accepted the emancipation of black people in rebel territory they would be pardoned. Lincoln's plan for rebuilding required only that a rebel state accept acts of Congress and presidential proclamations regarding slavery. Once 10 percent of its people eligible to vote in 1860 (white propertied males) said yes to these terms, a state could get on with reconstituting its government.

Lincoln had neither the clarity, the humanity, nor the resolve necessary to fix what was so fundamentally broken. Before the war he had opposed the expansion of slavery into the western territories, but he was never an abolitionist, never called for an *immediate* end to the abomination that was slavery.

Yes, in January 1863 Lincoln had issued the Emancipation Proclamation, declaring free black people who were held in rebel territory. But that was a military measure designed to increase the chaos in the Confederacy as more and more blacks made a mad dash to Union lines. The Emancipation Proclamation also allowed black men to serve in the Union's armed forces. Why? Because the Union was in desperate need of more soldiers.

Before Lincoln issued the Emancipation Proclamation, he had plotted to rid the nation of as many of the nearly half million free black people as possible. In this Lincoln was heavily influenced by two of his intellectual heroes.

One was Thomas Jefferson, who had advocated the expulsion of blacks from the United States in order to save the nation.

The other was Kentucky slaveholder and statesman Henry Clay. In 1816 Clay cofounded the American Colonization Society to encourage free blacks to leave the nation. Clay's society oversaw the resettlement of thousands in what is now Liberia, West Africa.

In Lincoln's resettlement plans he initially selected Chiriquí, a resource-poor area in what is today Panama.

Now if only the president could persuade black people to leave.

In August 1862, Lincoln summoned five of DC's black leaders to the White House. He told them it was their duty to accept immigration to South America given what their people had done to the United States. "But for your race among us there could not be war," said the president.

As to just how and why "your race" came to be "among us," Lincoln conveniently ignored that. His framing of the issue absolved slaveholders and their political allies of responsibility for catapulting the nation into a civil war. It also signaled the power of racism over patriotism.

Lincoln's anger in 1862 was directed at blacks who, by and large, fully supported the Union and did not want to leave the United States of America. Many would exclaim that, despite slavery and enforced poverty, "We will work, pray, live, and, if need be, die for the Union." Nevertheless, Lincoln cast black people as the enemy for wickedly dividing "us."

From this perspective flowed Lincoln's lack of clarity about the purpose and cause of the war. The president insisted that it was only about preserving the Union. Not about slavery!

Not about slavery?

The Confederacy operated under no such illusions. Its Senate president, R. M. T. Hunter, remarked, "What did we go to war for, but to protect our property?"

Not about slavery?

Mississippi's Articles of Secession stated unequivocally, "Our position is thoroughly identified with the institution of slavery. . . . Its labor supplies the product which constitutes by far the largest and most important portions of commerce of the earth."

Not about slavery?

Eighty-one percent of South Carolina's wealth was directly tied to owning human beings. Given Lincoln's opposition to the spread of slavery in the western territories, slaveholders had no reason to believe that he would stop there and wouldn't push to end slavery in the states, regardless of his statements to the contrary. No wonder South Carolina was willing to do whatever it took to be free from the federal government.

To cast the war as about something other than slavery, as Lincoln did—when in 1860 two-thirds of the wealthiest Americans lived in the slave states—to shroud that hard, cold reality under the cloak of "preserving the Union," would not and could not address the root causes of the war and the toll that centuries of slavery had wrought. And that failure of clarity led to a failure of humanity.

Millions upon millions of enslaved people had built the enormous wealth of the United States. During those nearly 250 years of unpaid toil, they had endured rape, whippings, murder, the dismemberment of families, and forced subjugation, illiteracy, and abject poverty. The quest to break the chains was clear at the start of the war when thousands of enslaved people escaped to Union forts and camps.

The drive for liberty led nearly two hundred thousand black men and boys—freeborn and once enslaved, the majority of them Southerners—to serve in the Union's armed forces. At war's end, humanity cried out to honor their sacrifice and heroism in service of the nation. Black people and their white allies believed that this military service *had* to carry with it citizenship rights and the dignity that comes from no black person being defined as property or legally inferior.

To be truly reborn this way, the United States needed to overcome not just a Southern but also a national disdain for black people. This disdain was horribly apparent during the New York City draft riots in the summer of 1863, when mobs of working-class whites, mostly Irishmen, went on a rampage against wealthy people, white abolitionists, and, most especially, black people.

"Black men and black women were attacked, but the rioters singled out the men for special violence," wrote Leslie M. Harris in her history of the black experience in early New York City, *In the Shadow of Slavery*. "On the waterfront, they hanged William Jones and then burned his body. White dock workers also beat and nearly drowned Charles Jackson, and they beat Jeremiah Robinson to death and threw his body in the river." This was not the worst of it.

"Rioters also made a sport of mutilating the black men's bodies, sometimes sexually. A group of white men and boys mortally attacked black sailor William Williams—jumping on his chest, plunging a knife into him, smashing his body with stones—while a crowd of men, women, and children watched."

This violence was simply the most overt, virulent expression of a stream of anti-black sentiment that constricted the lives of both the free and the enslaved. Every state admitted to the Union since 1819, starting with Maine, embedded in their constitutions discrimination against blacks, especially the denial of the right to vote. In addition, only Massachusetts did not exclude blacks from juries. Many states, from California to Ohio, prohibited blacks from testifying in court against someone who was white.

To combat what ailed the nation, something more radical, more muscular than Lincoln's Ten Percent Plan was sorely needed.

· · ·

Though Lincoln's lenient plan left 90 percent of the power in the South with those able to still openly dream of full-blown insurrection and consider themselves anything but loyal to the United States of America, blacks had cause for hope.

Several days after Lincoln issued that Proclamation of Amnesty and Reconstruction, on December 14, 1863, Representative James M. Ashley, a Republican from Ohio, and Senator John Henderson, a Democrat from Missouri, introduced in Congress an amendment to the Constitution abolishing chattel slavery: the Thirteenth Amendment. As with all amendments it needed to be ratified by three-fourths of the states to be adopted into the Constitution.

The Thirteenth Amendment passed in the US Senate in early April 1864, then in the US House of Representatives in late January 1865. It now had to be ratified by at least three-fourths of the states.

This Thirteenth Amendment was, in significant ways, revolutionary. By ending slavery through a US constitutional amendment, the Congress signaled it was willing to address civil rights at the federal level. This advocacy set the scene for the all-important Fourteenth and Fifteenth Amendments to follow.

The Thirteenth Amendment was also a corrective and an antidote for a Constitution whose drafters, like Thomas Jefferson, were overwhelmingly concerned with states' rights.

Finally, the amendment sought to give real meaning to "we hold these truths to be self-evident" by banning not just government-sponsored but also private agreements that exposed blacks to extralegal violence.

As then-congressman and future president James A. Garfield

THIRTEENTH AMENDMENT

SECTION 1
Neither slavery nor involuntary servitude, except as a punishment for crime whereof the party shall have been duly convicted, shall exist within the United States, or any place subject to their jurisdiction.

SECTION 2
Congress shall have power to enforce this article by appropriate legislation.

The entirety of the Thirteenth Amendment, which prohibits chattel slavery in the United States and its territories but allows for jails and prisons to force convicted criminals to work for no wages while in custody.

asked in a speech in Ravenna, Ohio, on the Fourth of July 1865, some six months after the passage of the Thirteenth Amendment, "What is Freedom? Is it a mere negation,—the bare privilege of not being chained, bought and sold, branded and scourged?" The Union army general and Republican then added, "If this is all, then freedom is a bitter mockery, a cruel delusion."

Passage of the Thirteenth Amendment bolstered black hope for justice. Shortly before this amendment cleared Congress, a group of black people in Tennessee (long since under Union control) issued a statement. They declared, in part: "We claim freedom, as our natural right, and ask that in harmony and co-operation with the nation at large, you should cut up by the roots the system of slavery, which is not only a wrong to us. . . . For slavery, corrupt itself, corrupted nearly all, also, around it, so that it has influenced nearly all the slave States to rebel against the Federal Government, in order to set up a government of pirates under which slavery might be perpetrated."

It was also in early 1865 that, as Confederate defeat loomed, a Union general's radical field order in Georgia, and some Congressional action, buoyed black hope even more.

Enslaved people outside the home of Confederate General Thomas F. Drayton in Hilton Head, South Carolina, in 1862. After the end of the Civil War came a host of new and harsh conditions for many black people in the South.

FORTY ACRES AND A MULE

IN JANUARY 1865, SHORTLY AFTER THE COMPLETION of his famous march to the sea and capture of Savannah, Georgia, the Union's general William Tecumseh Sherman issued Special Field Order No. 15, which, to take some of the pressure off his army, behind which thousands upon thousands had flocked during the march, set aside nearly four hundred thousand acres of land exclusively for black people.

This land, abandoned by Confederates, was in coastal South Carolina and Georgia (including their sea islands) and went as far south as Florida's St. Johns River. Each family was allowed up to forty acres (and though at one point the army gave people some surplus mules, no mules were ever promised).

General Sherman issued his Special Field Order No. 15 after he and Secretary of War Edwin McMasters Stanton met with twenty of Savannah's black clerics. The group's spokesman, Garrison Frazier, told the two white men that more than anything else his people wanted *Land! Land! Land!* Land on which to build independent, self-sufficient lives.

More good news came in March 1865: Congress created the Bureau of Refugees, Freedmen, and Abandoned Lands to aid needy blacks and whites in the South. This social service agency became known as the Freedmen's Bureau, because the majority of its clients were black people. The bureau's chief was Vermont native General Oliver O. Howard, an abolitionist. "Howard was neither a great administrator nor a great man," wrote activist-scholar W. E. B. Du Bois in his book *Black Reconstruction*, "but he was a good man. He was sympathetic and humane, and tried with endless application and desperate sacrifice to do a hard, thankless duty."

The Freedmen's Bureau distributed rations, operated schools, opened hospitals. It was also responsible for the reallocation of abandoned Southern land to the newly emancipated. The bureau's charge was to lease to up to forty acres of abandoned land to people who would have the option to buy that land after three years. Yes, once again, *land, land, land,* to provide economic self-sufficiency to a people who had endured hundreds of years of unpaid toil.

And history churned on.

April 9, 1865: General Robert E. Lee surrendered the Army of Northern Virginia—the Confederacy's main fighting force—to the general-in-chief of Union armies. This happened in the village of Appomattox Court House, Virginia.

April 14, 1865: Confederate sympathizer John Wilkes Booth shot President Lincoln in the head at DC's Ford Theatre.

April 15, 1865: Lincoln died a little after seven o'clock in the morning. Andrew Johnson of Tennessee, a Democrat like most Southerners at the time, was soon sworn in as president.

During the war, after the Union army had most of Tennessee in its control, Lincoln, a Republican, tapped Senator Johnson—fiercely loyal to the Union—to be Tennessee's military governor. Later, in Lincoln's second bid for the presidency, Johnson became his running mate. The Republican Party, calling itself the

THE REPUBLICAN VERSUS THE DEMOCRATIC PARTY

In the nineteenth century the Democratic Party supported the institution of slavery. The political party also advocated slavery's expansion into the western territories the United States acquired through purchase (the Louisiana Purchase in 1803) and war (the Mexican-American War, 1846–48). However, there was some debate within the Democratic Party. Southern Democrats wanted the spread of slavery to be unconditional. Northern Democrats favored popular sovereignty: allowing white settlers in new territories to decide whether or not slavery should be allowed on their soil.

The Republican Party formed in 1854 expressly to oppose the expansion of slavery into the western territories. Many Republicans were also abolitionists—advocates for the immediate end of slavery. Many Republicans also campaigned for black people to have the same rights that white people enjoyed. While most Republicans pushed for a strong, activist federal government, Democrats called for less federal government intervention and more states' rights.

The Democratic Party's and Republican Party's agendas and their constituencies would change in the twentieth century.

National Union Party during the war, thought that having a Southerner and a Democrat would, for one, make Lincoln more appealing to voters in the border states.

As Tennessee's military governor and as vice president Andrew Johnson blasted the Confederate leadership and plantation owners as "traitors" who "must be punished and impoverished." Johnson, who had grown up achingly poor, hardscrabble, and illiterate, utterly despised the Southern gentry who had challenged the Union.

His antipathy for the white aristocracy did not translate into support for black equality, however. In fact, this former slaveholder's contempt for black people was palpable.

Months after he became president, Johnson addressed a black DC regiment just back from service farther south. "Freedom is not simply the principle to live in idleness," Johnson chided the men. "Liberty does not mean merely to resort to the low saloons and other places of disreputable character."

Never mind that these were men who had honorably served the United States. Never mind that nearly two hundred thousand black men and boys had served in the Union's armed forces. Never mind that nearly forty thousand had died (most of disease) in this service.

In Johnson's estimation, blacks were just immoral, drunken sluggards.

Like many other whites, Johnson had maintained that the Civil War was only about preserving the Union. No more. No less. With that mind-set he set about stitching the rebel states back into the fabric of the nation.

First, within weeks of taking office—and with Congress *not* in session—on May 29, 1865, Johnson issued two proclamations. The first liberated most rebels from the charge of treason. All they had to do was swear loyalty to the Union and to the Constitution and "abide by and faithfully support all laws and proclamations which have been made during the existing rebellion with reference to the emancipation of slaves." Confederate leaders and rebels with real estate worth $20,000 or more had to appeal directly to Johnson for a pardon.

Soon, Johnson pardoned scores of former Confederates. He handed out full amnesty to thousands of white men whom he had called traitors.

Beneficiaries of Johnson's largesse included CSA vice president Alexander Stephens. Even more shocking to Republicans and black people keeping up with news, Johnson's generosity and forgiveness extended to a large number of wealthy plantation owners and other twenty-thousand-dollar men.

Johnson's second proclamation on May 29, 1865, revealed his plan for reunion. He began with North Carolina. Having appointed Democrat William Holden the Tar Heel State's provisional governor, Johnson ordered him to hold a new state constitutional convention. Johnson urged that this new constitution abolish slavery and that the state ratify the Thirteen Amendment. Johnson asked the same of other unreconstructed states.

Meanwhile, what exactly was going on down on the ground in the former Confederacy?

In the summer of 1865, at President Johnson's bequest, Union general Carl Schurz headed there to try to answer that question.

In his fact-finding mission Schurz toured Alabama, Georgia, Louisiana, Mississippi, and South Carolina. And what horrors he found!

Schurz recoiled as he gathered reports of black women who had been "scalped," had their "ears cut off," or had been thrown into a river and drowned amid chants for them to swim to the "damned Yankees."

Black boys and men were routinely stabbed, clubbed, and shot. Some were even "chained to a tree and burned to death." As he went from county to county, state to state, Schurz conveyed the sickening, unbearable stench of decomposing black bodies hanging from limbs, rotting in ditches, and clogging the roadways. White Southerners had unleashed a reign of terror that had reached "staggering proportions," wrote Annette Gordon-Reed in her biography of Andrew Johnson.

Many urged the president to strengthen the federal presence in the South. "Not only did Andrew Johnson preside over the country where this slow-motion genocide was taking place," wrote Gordon-Reed. "He strenuously resisted every effort to bring full protection to the people living under these conditions."

The president's failure to take action encouraged white Southerners, who recognized that they now had a friend in the White House.

Like a hydra, white supremacist regimes sprang out of Mississippi, Alabama, Georgia, and the other states of a newly resurgent South. As they drafted their new constitutions, the delegates were defiant, dismissive of any supposed federal authority, and ready to reassert and reimpose white supremacy.

At Louisiana's constitutional convention in October 1865,

delegates were so confident in the president's support and their reclaimed power that they resolved, "We hold this to be a Government of white people, made and to be perpetuated for the exclusive benefit of the white race; and in accordance with the constant adjudication of the United States Supreme Court." The Louisiana delegates concluded "that people of African descent cannot be considered as citizens of the United States." This was in line with the infamous US Supreme Court *Dred Scott* decision of 1857, wherein Chief Justice Roger B. Taney had stated explicitly that black people have "no rights which the white man is bound to respect."

Louisiana's declaration aligned perfectly with Johnson's. The United States is "a country for white men," Johnson had once declared, "and by God, as long as I'm President, it shall be a government for white men."

Years later, former Confederate secretary of the treasury Christopher Memminger confessed that at war's end the Confederacy, so destroyed, so broken, so bereft, would have done just about anything the North asked in order to get back into the Union. But then, said Memminger, President Johnson "held up before us the hope of 'a white man's government.'"

One Georgia plantation owner agreed as he asserted that white Southerners now had "the right and power to govern our population in our own way."

Mississippi showed the way.

Many editorial cartoons of the time noted that the governmental policies of Reconstruction—and of President Andrew Johnson in particular—favored white citizens at the expense of black people.

BLACK CODES

IN THE FALL OF 1865, MISSISSIPPI PASSED A SERIES of laws to control black people. As Du Bois noted, these notorious Black Codes "were an astonishing affront to emancipation" and made "plain and indisputable" the "attempt on the part of the Southern states to make Negroes slaves in everything but name."

These Codes required black people to sign annual labor contracts with plantation, mill, or mine owners. If black people refused or could show no proof of gainful employment, they would be charged with vagrancy and put on the auction block, with their labor sold to the highest bidder. The supposed contract was beyond binding. It was more like a shackle.

Blacks were forbidden to seek better wages and working conditions with another employer. No matter how horrible the working conditions, if they left the plantation, lumber camp, or mine, they would be jailed and auctioned off. They were trapped.

Self-sufficiency itself was illegal. Black people couldn't hold any other employment besides laborer or domestic (unless they had the written consent of the mayor or judge). They were also banned from hunting and fishing, and thus denied the means even to stave off hunger. More galling yet was a provision whereby black children who had been sold before the war and hadn't yet reunited with their parents were to be apprenticed off. Their former masters had the first right to their labor.

And if black people protested all these indignities?

The penalty for defiance, insulting gestures, and inappropriate behavior, the Black Codes made clear, was a no-holds-barred whipping. Mississippi's success in re-creating slavery was undeniable. With the exception of Arkansas, the former Confederate states quickly copied Mississippi's Black Codes, sometimes verbatim.

Under Florida's Black Codes, disobedience or impudence was a "form of vagrancy, and a vagrant could be whipped," as detailed in A. J. Langguth's *After Lincoln*. In Louisiana black adults had to sign labor contracts within "the first ten days of each year that committed them and their children to work on a plantation." In North Carolina "orphans were sent to work for the former masters of their families rather than allowing them to live with grandparents or other relatives."

"If you call this Freedom what do you call Slavery?" wrote Henry Mars of Shelbyville, Kentucky, to Secretary of War Stanton in May 1866.

To stop this descent into the cauldrons of racial hate, black men had to have access to the ballot box. The reasoning was simple. As long as they were disenfranchised, white politicians could continue to ignore or, even worse, trample on black people and suffer absolutely no electoral consequences for doing so. The moment black men had the vote, elected officials risked being ousted for spewing anti-black rhetoric and promoting racially discriminatory policies. (At this time most people, including many women, were not concerned with a woman's right to vote.)

Black male suffrage as a requirement for a state's readmission had been a glaring, fatal omission in President Lincoln's vision for Reconstruction and in that of Andrew Johnson, who further revealed his lack of compassion, his hatred for black people in October 1865: he revoked General Sherman's Special Field Order No. 15. Most of the four hundred thousand acres of Low Country land that had been set aside for black people would revert back to former rebels. Some forty-thousand black people had begun to work and build lives, new communities in the region.

Not surprisingly, Andrew Johnson was not troubled in the least by the Black Codes.

Not even Union general (and future president) Ulysses S. Grant saw anything wrong with the Black Codes. Despite all brutal evidence to the contrary, Grant was convinced that white Southerners had adjusted well to losing the Civil War. To Grant's mind, if black people resisted and complained bitterly about the Black Codes, it could mean only one thing: the Freedmen's Bureau was "encouraging unrealistic expectations among the former slaves," *After Lincoln* explained.

In November 1865, one Philadelphia newspaper, the white-owned *North American and United States Gazette*, a hair more realistic, acknowledged the odiousness of the Black Codes but found them necessary nonetheless. Perhaps the form they took was a touch too severe, but the Black Codes, it argued, were not about trying to reestablish slavery. The Southern states "just wanted to stop vagrancy and put an end to the undeniable evils of idleness and pauperism arising from the sudden emancipation of so many slaves." By compelling them to work, the argument went, this measure prevented the newly freed from becoming a "burden upon society."

What the paper failed to recognize was that black people's willingness to work had never been the problem. Having to work for free, under backbreaking conditions and the threat of the lash, was the real issue. Nor did Johnson's policies or the Black Codes ensure that black people would not be a "burden upon society." If anything, they guaranteed the opposite. Blacks were by and large denied access to land, banned from hunting and fishing, and forbidden to work independently using skills honed and developed while enslaved, such as blacksmithing. Under such conditions, how could people become self-sufficient?

The bottom line was that black economic independence was anathema to a power structure that depended on cheap, exploitable, rightless labor and required black subordination. But instead of homing in on this fundamental reality, the Philadelphia newspaper simply bemoaned the unforeseen and unfortunate consequences of the Black Codes for whites. It complained that, since "planters refuse to pay wages at all" to black people due to the landowners' claims that, "negroes are so lazy as not to be worth paying," there was a downward pressure on overall wages that left poor whites unable to find work that provided enough "to keep soul and body together."

Yet, Johnson reveled in the charge that he was "too much of the poor man's friend." But then, when it seemed that the only way to keep blacks as labor without rights was to reinstate the leadership of the old Confederacy, Johnson essentially threw his core constituency under the bus: whites first impoverished under the old plantocracy, then treated as cannon fodder during the war, were now economic roadkill on the way to reasserting "slavery by another name."

Another article in that same issue of *North American and United States Gazette* asserted that the South was in much better shape than could have been expected, and this was because of the president's policies, which were "worthy of our admiration." Johnson understood that the "war was for the Union, and the Union has been restored beyond our most sanguine expectations." The president, then, was to be commended for a "job well done."

Andrew Johnson's message to Congress on December 4, 1865, had that same upbeat, triumphal cadence: The war was over. The South was repentant. New governments had been formed. The federal government, he concluded, had done what it had set out to do and done it beautifully. He had heard some rumblings about voting and civil rights for black people, but any lingering questions about rights, Johnson felt, were matters for the states.

How stunning, too, that such a prideful, stubborn man swallowed his dignity over and over again when states he had just welcomed back into the fold defied even the very low standards he had set to rejoin the United States of America.

South Carolina ratified the Thirteenth Amendment only after the state had attached a declaration with its own series of "if, then, but" clauses nullifying any federal right to enforce the antislavery provision. To make its point perfectly clear, the state also refused to renounce its Articles of Secession.

Louisiana and Alabama attached their own addenda negating congressional authority over the status of slavery within their borders.

When Johnson declared the Union restored in December 1865, Florida had not ratified the amendment. Neither had Texas and Mississippi. Such was Mississippi's obstinacy that it did not officially ratify the Thirteenth Amendment until 2013.

In the end, with the half-hearted, tarnished ratifications of some former Confederate states, on December 6, 1865, the necessary three-fourths of the Union's states—twenty-seven of its thirty-six—had ratified the Thirteenth Amendment. It officially became part of the Constitution on December 18. The abolition of slavery was about the only thing black people and progressive white people had to celebrate.

Because of Johnson's rash of pardons, the rebel states' new governments looked hauntingly like those from the Old South. When it came to the US Senate and House of Representatives, for example, the CSA vice president Stephens and cabinet officers, as well as ten Confederate generals, a number of colonels, and nearly sixty Confederate Congress representatives were ready to be ensconced in the nation's capital.

As the president surveyed all that he had accomplished, he was satisfied. He simply could not fathom that Northern Republicans, concerned about the complete deprivation of rights for black people, would criticize or try to undo what he had so painstakingly stitched together.

Andrew Johnson was dead wrong.

The Freedmen's Bureau, an agency that primarily helped black people, faced fierce criticism as opponents claimed it raised unrealistic expectations of how blacks should be treated in a postwar South.

5

"WE SHOWED OUR HAND TOO SOON"

FOR MANY NORTHERN CONGRESSMEN, THE BLACK Codes sparked a general sense of outrage.

Voluminous testimony about whippings, killings, and virtual slavery were all too much for them to stomach, especially the Radical Republicans, men such as Massachusetts senator Charles Sumner and Pennsylvania representative Thaddeus Stevens.

The sight of unrepentant leaders of the Confederacy, such as General Benjamin Humphreys, now Mississippi governor, in power was infuriating.

Andrew Johnson's audacity to rebuild the nation without even the advice and counsel of the legislative branch was absolutely unacceptable.

For Congress, the core issue was the newly emancipated. Without any rights, without any citizenship, they would be left without any hope. They would be at the mercy of the old slavocracy.

When Congress was back in session in December 1865, it

refused to seat recently elected senators and representatives from the former Confederate states. These states would be on ice until a congressional Joint Committee on Reconstruction conducted an investigation to decide if and on what terms they should be readmitted.

"We showed our hand too soon," said a regretful Mississippi planter speaking of the Black Codes. "We ought to have waited till the troops were withdrawn, and our representatives admitted to Congress; then we could have had everything our own way." He was right.

Radical Republicans sought for black people a sweeping agenda—land, citizenship, and the vote (and that is what made them "radical"). However, the majority of Congress was not willing to go that far.

Moderate Republicans did believe, however, that Johnson had not gone far enough. At a bare minimum, citizenship needed to be fully acknowledged. Also, the Freedmen's Bureau, which by law was set to shut its doors in April 1866, had to continue setting up schools for the newly freed. When freedom came, just a little more than 3 percent of the four million formerly enslaved people were literate. Congressmen also wanted the bureau to have jurisdiction in the old Confederacy over cases where black people were not getting the equal protection of the laws.

In early February 1866, Congress passed the Freedmen's Bureau Bill and then, in early March, the Civil Rights Bill, which defined as citizens all persons born in the United States, except for Native Americans living in unsettled territory and on reservations. At one point the Civil Rights Bill contained clauses on black suffrage and land distribution. The moderates had stripped those clauses out, believing they would be the only ones that would get Johnson's back up. Once those clauses were gone moderates were certain that the president would easily sign both bills into law.

They were wrong.

So venomous was Johnson's veto of the Freedmen's Bureau Bill that it left even his supporters in Congress stunned.

He railed against the unconstitutionality of the legislation, given that eleven rebel states, despite their newly formed governments, were not represented in Congress.

He denounced the creation of a judicial system under the Freedmen's Bureau when there were perfectly good courts already in existence in the South.

He raged against the beginnings of a bloated federal bureaucracy designed to tend to the needs of "one class of people" while ignoring "our own race." He demanded to know why the government would build schools for blacks when it did not even do that for whites. Johnson further lectured that the modest land provision still in existence from Sherman's Special Field Order No. 15 was just plain wrong and set a horrible precedent. The government "never deemed itself authorized to expend the public money for the rent or purchase of homes for the thousands, not to say millions, of the white race who are honestly toiling from day to day for their subsistence," so why would it do so for the freedmen? This bill, he was convinced, was designed to set up black dependency on the federal government. And he was having none of it.

The president, despite evidence to the contrary, concurred

with his advisers that "the current condition of a freedman was 'not so bad.'"

"His condition is not so exposed as may at first be imagined," said the president in his veto. "He is in a portion of the country where his labor cannot well be spared. Competition for his services from planters, from those who are constructing or repairing railroads, or from capitalists in his [vicinity], or from other States, will enable him to command almost his own terms." The president also claimed that the black man had "a perfect right to change his place of abode," that he could pull up stakes and move to a place "where labor is more esteemed and better rewarded."

Johnson insisted that the "laws that regulate supply and demand will maintain their force, and the wages of the laborer will be regulated thereby."

What's more, given that black people didn't have it so bad, Johnson saw no reason they could not build their own schools and buy their own land instead of waiting for a handout from the government. "It is earnestly hoped that instead of wasting away, they will, by their own efforts, establish for themselves a condition of respectability and prosperity."

Ludicrous.

No, the black man did not have "a perfect right to change his place of abode" in search of a better job. Not unless he wanted to risk being arrested on vagrancy charges and auctioned off. By and large, black men (and women) could not use their skills for anything but cleaning plantation owners' houses, picking cotton, chopping sugarcane, or planting tobacco and rice. The laws of supply and demand—Johnson's alleged cure-all—could not operate.

His determination to see to it that this was "a white man's government" had undercut not only democracy but the basic tenets of capitalism as well.

That same hypocrisy was evident in Johnson's vision of land ownership.

While claiming that the government had never provided access to land for white folks, Johnson simply erased the nineteen years that he had worked for the passage of the Homestead Act (1862), which *gave*, not leased, 160 acres of land wrested or browbeaten from Native Americans in the West. And Johnson hadn't stopped with the Homestead Act.

During the war, in 1864, he advocated taking the plantation owners' land as well and distributing it to poor white farmers, whose opportunities, he felt, had been denied and whose chances had been thwarted by the enslaved and the slaveholders alike.

Meanwhile, Johnson cringed that the formerly enslaved would lease forty acres abandoned by those whom he had once called traitors. Perhaps this disparity in treatment reflected Johnson's wish to reward those who embodied the "good old American work ethic." The truth was much more complicated.

When, as a teenager in Mississippi, future president of the Confederacy Jefferson Davis had refused to go to school, his father sent him into the cotton fields. But he did not last long. "After the boy spent two days stooping under the Mississippi sun, the classroom became more appealing," wrote Langguth in *After Lincoln*.

Shortly after the war, the *North American and United States Gazette* reported that "all northern men visiting" the South had one "universal complaint": "White men are as averse to labor as ever. Rich or poor, they all ignore work."

Similarly, Schurz, the Union general who toured the South, reported that in his conversation with a plantation owner, who was beside himself that emancipation had left him without any slaves to do the heavy lifting, the man dismissed the idea of working the land himself. "The idea that he would work with his hands as a farmer seemed to strike him as ludicrously absurd. He told me with a smile that he had never done a day's work of that kind in his life."

Nonetheless, Johnson had absolutely no qualms about using the power of government to ensure that plantation owners and poor whites gained or regained title to millions of acres of land, whereas those who had actually labored hard in the vast fields were treated as criminals and vagrants who needed the threat of the whip in order to work.

The president's concerns about a proposed judicial system where freed people might be able to find some justice for the violence raining down on them were equally ridiculous—and dangerous.

Johnson insisted that the existing court structure was fair, equitable, and fully functioning. However, Southern courts were "racist, biased, obstructionist, and oblivious to northern opinion," explained Michael A. Ross in his book *Justice of Shattered Dreams*. "Southern judges and law enforcement officials . . . looked the other way when ex-rebels committed violent crimes against blacks and white Unionists, (white Southerners who had not supported the Confederacy). State courts forbade testimony by blacks, making crimes against African Americans nearly impossible to prove. Black veterans of the Union army were particular targets of unpunished violence."

Black people most definitely needed the Freedmen's Bureau's judicial system because the Southern courts in place were designed to provide legal cover for terror against them.

For one.

A second function of Southern courts was to enslave black people through the convict-lease system. The instrument of re-enslavement was a brutal deployment of sheriffs, judges, and hard-labor punishment for black-only offenses such as carrying a firearm, making an insulting gesture, or stealing a pig. Black people were then swept into the prison system and parceled out to slave away on a local or state public-works project (such as a railroad) or for plantation, mine, and lumber mill owners.

These convicts received paltry sustenance, such as food. Those who died working the fields or in the mines could be easily replaced by more black bodies charged with vagrancy and handed a death sentence.

As for Johnson's fury over the government providing schools for black children when it had never done that for white children, to be sure, the South did not have a tradition of public schooling for anyone, least of all poor whites or blacks. "The planters believed that state government had no right to intervene in the education of children and, by extension, the larger social arrangement," explained James D. Anderson in *The Education of Blacks in the South, 1860–1935*.

Why would the ruling elite—many of whom hired private tutors for their children—not want *all* white children to have an education?

As in most oppressive societies, those in power knew that an educated population would only upset the political and economic order.

Of course, black literacy had been actively forbidden before the Civil War. Many black people paid dearly for daring to learn to read and write. In one case, wrote Anderson, "a slave by the name of Scipio was put to death for teaching a slave child how to read and spell, and the child was severely beaten to make him 'forget what he had learned.'"

After the war, the South remained dead set against black literacy. Thomas Conway, Freedmen's Bureau assistant commissioner for Louisiana, warned his boss, General Howard, that whites had made it clear that all that stood between them and stripping blacks of any hope of land and education was a thin line of Union troops. Conway ominously added that if the soldiers were removed, black schools would be the first thing to vanish.

As for Andrew Johnson, he remained adamant that if black people wanted schools, they would have to build their own.

This is precisely what black people had been doing. One Freedmen's Bureau official recorded that all over the South "an effort is being made by the colored people to educate themselves." He reckoned that there were "at least 500 schools" built, staffed, and run by black people in 1866.

Although many poor whites languished, refusing to attend schools built under what many likely called "darky programs" of the Freedmen's Bureau, the formerly enslaved emerged "with a fundamentally different consciousness of literacy," stated Anderson. Such people saw "reading and writing as a contradiction of oppression."

Instead of offering any support to those who embodied the self-reliance he said he valued, Johnson was blind to the herculean and impressive effort that blacks had mounted in the South. Instead, he demanded they do even more without any help.

President Johnson also raged against the Civil Rights Bill of 1866. He argued that black people had to *earn* their citizenship. In his veto, he reminded Congress that black people had just emerged from slavery and, therefore, "should pass through a certain probation . . . before attaining the coveted prize." They had to "give evidence of their fitness to receive and to exercise the rights of citizens." For Johnson, nearly 250 years of unpaid toil to build one of the wealthiest nations on earth did not earn citizenship.

Also, he feared that the Civil Rights Bill would "establish for the security of the colored race safeguards which go infinitely beyond any that the General Government has ever provided for the white race." He continued: "the bill [is] made to operate in favor of the colored and against the white race." The Civil Rights Bill, a simple injunction against discriminating against blacks, was labeled as favoritism—and that is what made the proposed legislation so patently unacceptable to him. The bill, Johnson complained, was just the opening salvo in the Radical Republicans' efforts to "protect" Negros.

Congress overrode both of Johnson's vetoes and hoped there might be some way to work with the president. But in the spring and summer of 1866, the South's descent into an orgy of antiblack violence signaled the final break between Johnson and the Republicans.

THE RIOT IN NEW ORLEANS—MURDERING NEGROES IN THE REAR OF MECHANICS' INSTITUTE.
[SKETCHED BY THEODORE R. DAVIS.]

New Orleans was the site of a violent outburst in 1866 after Radical Republicans met to discuss granting blacks the right to vote; nearly fifty blacks were killed. President Johnson's silence after the act was an implicit endorsement of the anti-black violence running rampant through the country at that time.

THE RIOT IN NEW ORLEANS—PLATFORM IN MECHANICS' INSTITUTE AFTER THE RIOT.
[SKETCHED BY THEODORE R. DAVIS.]

"JOHNSON IS WITH US!"

IN EARLY MAY 1866 A WHITE ASSAULT ON BLACK settlements in Memphis, Tennessee, left more than forty black people and two white people dead and numerous black homes, churches, and schools in ashes.

After Memphis, silence from the White House.

In late July there was another gory bloodbath in New Orleans, Louisiana. Nearly fifty blacks were slaughtered and more than a hundred injured for meeting to discuss voting. When one member of the white mob, who had just bludgeoned a black man to death, was warned that "he might be punished," he scoffed. "Oh, hell! Haven't you seen the papers?" he said. "Johnson is with us!"

After New Orleans, another of round of silence from the White House.

As the black body count mounted, justice was nowhere to be found, least of all from the president of the United States.

Congress, therefore, moved to provide some level of protection with several Reconstruction acts. The first and major one came in March 1867. It reduced the former Confederate states—except for Tennessee—to conquered territories. The ten states were put under military rule in five military districts. In these districts some twenty thousand federal troops stood between a still-smoldering, vengeful rebel population and black people.

The ten states had to yet again hold new state constitutional conventions—but this time black men could not be barred from serving as delegates. This time new state constitutions had to include the black man's right to vote. The terms of a state's readmission included Congressional approval of its new constitution. More important: the state had to ratify the Fourteenth Amendment, which had cleared Congress back in June 1866.

Through the Fourteenth Amendment black people became American *citizens* and citizens of their states. States were forbidden to move against the "privileges and immunities" of black or any other citizens: that is, Kentucky could not treat a citizen of Boston in a discriminatory manner (and vice versa). States were also banned from depriving *anyone* of life, liberty, or property without "due process," that is a fair day in court. Nor could states deny *anyone* "the equal protection of the laws," that is, a police officer ought not arrest a black person for robbing a white person, but look the other way when a white person robbed a black person.

What's more, the amendment pressured states to recognize that black men had the right to vote. For a state's representation in Congress would be based on the number of *all* its men ages twenty-one and up, not just white men eligible to vote.

Tennessee had ratified the Fourteenth Amendment back in the summer of 1866, which is why it was not put under military rule.

The demands Congress made of former Confederate states resulted in black people finally being able to participate in American democracy. Take South Carolina, where in 1860 more than 50 percent of the population was black. At its state constitutional convention under Congressional Reconstruction, about 60 percent of the 124 delegates were men of African descent. Along with their white colleagues, these men called for free public school for *all* young people (something that did not happen right away, however). Many of the black delegates went on to become state legislators and hold other offices, such as postmaster and sheriff, as did hundreds and hundreds of blacks who attended other state constitutional conventions. And the way was paved for black men to serve in the US Congress.

On July 9, 1868, the Fourteenth Amendment was ratified. It was adopted into the Constitution on July 28. A year and a half later, on February 3, 1870, democracy was honored, respected once more. On this date the Fifteenth Amendment, through which black men were granted the national vote, was ratified.

Legions of white people in the South were none too pleased with these civil rights developments. The backlash kept apace in the form of hate-filled rants, intimidation, and savage violence.

In response to the rising tide of white-on-black shotgun blasts, stabbings, thrashings, whippings, and murders by the Ku Klux Klan and other white paramilitary terrorist groups, beginning in May 1870, Congress issued several Enforcement acts, known as "force acts." With these laws came penalties for interfering with or depriving people of their Fourteenth and Fifteenth

FOURTEENTH AMENDMENT

SECTION 1

All persons born or naturalized in the United States, and subject to the jurisdiction thereof, are citizens of the United States and of the State wherein they reside. No State shall make or enforce any law which shall abridge the privileges or immunities of citizens of the United States; nor shall any State deprive any person of life, liberty, or property, without due process of law; nor deny to any person within its jurisdiction the equal protection of the laws.

SECTION 2

Representatives shall be apportioned among the several States according to their respective numbers, counting the whole number of persons in each State, excluding Indians not taxed. But when the right to vote at any election for the choice of electors for President and Vice-President of the United States, Representatives in Congress, the Executive and Judicial officers of a State, or the members of the Legislature thereof, is denied to any of the male inhabitants of such State, being twenty-one years of age, and citizens of the United States, or in any way abridged, except for participation in rebellion, or other crime, the basis of representation therein shall be reduced in the proportion which the number of such male citizens shall bear to the whole number of male citizens twenty-one years of age in such State.

SECTION 3

No person shall be a Senator or Representative in Congress, or elector of President and Vice-President, or hold any office, civil or military, under the United States, or under any State, who, having previously taken an oath, as a member of Congress, or as an officer of the United States, or as a member of any State legislature, or as an executive or judicial officer of any State, to support the Constitution of the United States, shall have engaged in insurrection or rebellion against the same, or given aid or comfort to the enemies thereof. But Congress may by a vote of two-thirds of each House, remove such disability.

SECTION 4

The validity of the public debt of the United States, authorized by law, including debts incurred for payment of pensions and bounties for services in suppressing insurrection or rebellion, shall not be questioned. But neither the United States nor any State shall assume or pay any debt or obligation incurred in aid of insurrection or rebellion against the United States, or any claim for the loss or emancipation of any slave; but all such debts, obligations and claims shall be held illegal and void.

SECTION 5

The Congress shall have the power to enforce, by appropriate legislation, the provisions of this article.

The entirety of the Fourteenth Amendment. Because of **SECTION 1**, *with its definition of citizenship and its prohibitions on states abusing people capriciously, the Fourteenth Amendment is cited in more lawsuits than any other amendment.*

SECTION 2 counters the Constitution's original dictate that an enslaved person be counted as three-fifths of a person when it came to tallying up how many representatives a state was entitled to have. This was a compromise on the issue of basing representation on population. Nonslave states had not wanted enslaved people to be counted at all in order to reduce the number of representatives a slave state would have. Slave states had wanted enslaved people counted as whole persons to increase their number of representatives. In making male eligible voters the basis of congressional apportionment, the amendment essentially denied women the right to vote.

SECTION 3 aimed to prevent former rebels from holding public office.

SECTION 4 was another blow for the former Confederacy: the United States would not be responsible for any debt those states incurred during the rebellion.

SECTION 5 emphasized that civil rights legislation would be pursued at a federal, not state, level.

THE FIFTEENTH AMENDMENT

SECTION 1
The right of citizens of the United States to vote shall not be denied or abridged by the United States or by any State on account of race, color, or previous condition of servitude.

SECTION 2
The Congress shall have the power to enforce this article by appropriate legislation.

With the simple lack of considering gender, the Fifteenth Amendment left the door wide open for voting rights to be denied or curtailed on account of sex. American women would not receive the right to the national vote until 1920, through the Nineteenth Amendment.

Amendment rights. What's more, the president was authorized to use federal troops to combat terrorism.

With the force acts, with the Fourteenth Amendment, with the Fifteenth Amendment, Congress created a legal structure to begin to atone for the "original sin" of a fractured nation—one tenuously restored through congressional Reconstruction on July 15, 1870, the date Georgia became the tenth state under military rule to be readmitted to the Union.

Morrison R. Waite served as chief justice of the US Supreme Court from 1874–88. During this time, he oversaw cases that asserted strict literal readings of the Thirteenth, Fourteenth, and Fifteenth Amendments that limited the scope of rights guaranteed to black people.

COURTING JUSTICE

IN HIS THIRD AUTOBIOGRAPHY, *THE LIFE AND Times of Frederick Douglass*, the great man lamented that by the time the justices had finished, "in most of the Southern States, the fourteenth and fifteenth amendments are virtually nullified. The rights which they were intended to guarantee are denied and held in contempt. The citizenship granted in the fourteenth amendment is practically a mockery, and the right to vote . . . is literally stamped out in face of government." This autobiography was published in 1892, three years before Fredrick Douglass died. The justices to whom he referred were the all-male, all-white members of the US Supreme Court.

The US Supreme Court justices gave the aura of being "strict constitutionalists," that is, jurists who did not interpret or create but merely distinguished between the rights the federal government enforced and those controlled by the states. But the supposedly legally neutral interpretations had profound effects. And the court, just like Johnson, demonstrated an uncanny ability to ignore inconsistencies and to twist rules, beliefs, and values to undermine the solid progress in black people's rights that the Radical Republicans had finally managed to put in place.

The court declared that the Reconstruction amendments—the Thirteenth, Fourteenth, and Fifteenth—had illegally placed the full scope of civil rights, which had once been so strictly the domain of states, under federal authority. The court essentially held that the federal government had made a power grab. That, said the court, was unconstitutional. It put the states under the federal government's thumb, disrupted the distribution of power in the federal system, and radically altered the framework of American government. The justices consistently held to this reading of the Constitution when it came to the rights of black people. The ruling that began this long, disastrous legal retreat from a rights-based society was the *Slaughterhouse Cases*.

Back in 1869, given New Orleans's susceptibly to cholera and yellow fever, the Louisiana state legislature passed a law that confined butcher shops, with their blood, entrails, and inevitable disease, to a discrete section of the city, on the premises of a newly created corporation: Crescent City Livestock Landing & Slaughterhouse Company. Butchers who wanted to continue to pen, sell, and slaughter their cattle, hogs, and other livestock had to also pay fees to this company.

Several hundred butchers cried foul and went to court. Was not being compelled to work at Crescent City Livestock Landing & Slaughterhouse "involuntary servitude"—a violation of the Thirteenth Amendment?

Had they not been deprived of "privileges or immunities" without "due process"? Where was their equal protection of the laws? Was this not a violation of the Fourteenth Amendment?

Wrong and wrong, ruled the US Supreme Court in its 5–4 decisions on April 14, 1873. The justices ruled that the Thirteenth Amendment was about ending the enslavement of people of African descent.

As for the Fourteenth Amendment, it covered only federal citizenship rights, such as the right to peaceful assembly and habeas corpus (Latin for "you should have the body"), a person's right to not be kept in prison without being brought before a court of law to determine if there was cause for confinement. Everything else—such as a right to ply one's trade—said the ruling, came under the domain of the states. As Ross put it in *Justice of Shattered Dreams*, "citizens still had to seek protection for most of their civil rights from state governments and state courts."

Even the right to vote, despite the Fifteenth Amendment, was not federally protected in the eyes of the US Supreme Court. One case that bore this out was *United States v. Reese* (1875). It involved William Garner, a black man in Lexington, Kentucky, who had tried to vote in the 1873 local elections. The registrars, Hiram Reese and Matthew Foushee, refused to hand Garner a ballot because he had not paid a poll tax of $1.50. Yet the black man had an affidavit that the tax collector had refused to accept his payment. The registrars scoffed. With one wing of local government demanding proof of payment and the other flat-out refusing to accept the funds, Garner knew his right to vote had been violated.

The US Supreme Court, in an 8–1 decision, disagreed.

Chief Justice Morrison R. Waite wrote that the Fifteenth Amendment did not guarantee the right to vote but, as Bruce R. Trimble summed up in his biography of Waite, the Fifteenth Amendment "had merely prevented the states from giving preference to one citizen over another on account of race, color, etc." To emphasize the point, Waite reiterated, the "right to vote . . . comes from the states."

In quick succession, the court had undermined citizenship, due process, and the right to vote. Next was the basic right to live.

In 1873, Southern Democrats, angered that black Americans had voted in a Republican government in Colfax, Louisiana, threatened to overturn the results of the recent election and install a white supremacist regime. Blacks were determined to defend their citizenship rights and occupied the symbol of democracy in Colfax: the courthouse. They sought to ensure that the duly elected representatives, most of whom were white Republicans, could take office.

That act of democratic courage resulted in an unprecedented bloodbath, even for Reconstruction. Depending on the casualty estimate, between 105 and 280 blacks were slaughtered. Their killers were then charged with violating the Enforcement Act of 1870, which Congress had passed to stop the Klan's terrorism.

In this case, *United States v. Cruikshank*, decided on March 24, 1876, Chief Justice Waite ruled that the Enforcement Act violated states' rights. Moreover, the only recourse the federal government could take was the Fourteenth Amendment, but, he continued, that did not cover vigilantes or private acts of terror, but rather covered only acts of violence carried out by states. The ruling not only let mass murderers go free, it effectively removed the ability of the federal government to rein in anti-black domestic terrorism.

A year after *United States v. Cruikshank* was decided, Reconstruction was over. It ended after the wildly controversial presidential election of 1876. The Republican candidate was Rutherford B. Hayes, governor of Ohio. The Democratic candidate was Samuel Tilden, governor of New York.

On election night, November 7, 1876, there was no clear winner. Twenty electoral votes were in dispute. There were charges of fraud from both sides. Not even after the Electoral College met in early December 1876 was there a resolution. And not after a special Electoral Commission convened in late January 1877, either.

Then came a clandestine meeting between representatives of both parties in late February 1877, at a luxurious hotel owned by a black man, James Wormley.

A deal was struck over many things. Chief among them was this: Hayes could have the presidency if he agreed to remove the remaining troops stationed in the South, in South Carolina and Louisiana.

On March 4, 1877, Rutherford B. Hayes became the nation's nineteenth president. Before April was out, those federal troops in the two states were withdrawn. The steady retreat from protecting blacks' rights was now in full force.

The following year in *Hall v. DeCuir* (1878), the justices ruled that a state could not prohibit racial segregation.

Then, in a series of decisions—*Strauder v. West Virginia* (1880), *Ex parte Virginia* (1880), and *Virginia v. Rives* (1880)—the US Supreme

Court provided clear guidelines to the states on how to systematically and constitutionally exclude black Americans from juries in favor of white jurors.

But the rollback of rights was not over yet.

Next on the list: dignity and equality.

Back on March 1, 1875, black Americans and their white allies had celebrated the Civil Rights Act of 1875. It made it illegal to discriminate against people in places of public accommodation, such as restaurants and trains. Doing so could result in imprisonment for a year and a thousand-dollar fine.

In the *Civil Rights Cases* (1883), the justices ruled that the 1875 Civil Rights Act was unconstitutional because the Fourteenth Amendment could be enforced only by the states, not the federal government. Moreover, in a wicked one-two punch, the justices added that the Thirteenth Amendment's ban on "badges of servitude" did not extend to discrimination in public accommodations.

US Supreme Court associate justice Joseph Bradley was exasperated with black Americans consistently seeking legal redress and laws to fend off the violence, state-sponsored discrimination, legalized terror, and the reimposition of what Professor William M. Wiecek has called "crypto-slavery" and a "netherworld of rightlessness" that had come to define their lives after the Civil War. Judge Bradley barked that "there must be some stage in the progress of his elevation when [the black man] takes the rank of a mere citizen, and ceases to be the special favorite of the laws." Like Andrew Johnson, Bradley saw equal treatment for black people as favoritism. Unequal treatment, however, became the law of the land.

For white supremacists, the crowning glory was *Plessy v. Ferguson.*

Homer Plessy, a black man who looked white, thought his challenge to a Louisiana law that forced him to ride in the Jim Crow railcar instead of the one designated for whites would put an end to this legal descent into black subjugation.

He was wrong.

On May 18, 1896, the justices, in an 8–1 decision, dismissed the claims that Plessy's Fourteenth Amendment rights to equal protection under the law were violated. Justice Henry Brown unequivocally stated, "If one race be inferior to the other socially, the constitution of the United States cannot put them on the same plane."

As for the argument that segregation violated the Thirteenth Amendment's ban against "badges of servitude," the Supreme Court shot down that down as well, noting: "We consider the underlying fallacy of [Plessy's] argument . . . to consist in the assumption that the enforced separation of the two races stamps the colored race with a badge of inferiority. If this be so, it is not by reason of anything found in the act, but solely because the colored race chooses to put that construction upon it."

Despite more than a generation of irrefutable evidence of widespread racial discrimination in the aftermath of the Civil War, the court created the mythic "separate but equal" doctrine to confirm racial segregation as the law of the land.

The court then followed up with a ruling in *Cumming v. Richmond County Board of Education* (1899) that even ignored *Plessy's* separate but equal doctrine. For the court declared that in the case of impending financial crisis, it was perfectly acceptable to shut down black schools while continuing to operate schools for white children.

Just prior to that, the court had sanctioned closing off the ballot box.

In a unanimous 9–0 decision in *Williams v. Mississippi* (1898), the justices approved the use of the poll tax: the requirement for eligible voters to pay a fee to register to vote. Although the discriminatory intent of the requirement was well known prior to the justices' ruling, the highest court in the land sanctioned this formidable barrier to the ballot box.

The repercussions were harrowing for American democracy. The poll tax not only ensnared black voters but also trapped poor whites. As late as 1942, for instance, only 3 percent of the voting-age population cast a ballot in seven poll tax states. Just *3 percent* of an electorate in these states decided who would sit in the US Senate and House of Representatives to shape federal policy.

This, in turn, strengthened the years of seniority and thus the stranglehold on federal law of these officials, who accordingly rose in the ranks to assume or hold on to key leadership positions, such as chairing the Foreign Relations Committee, judiciary committees, and others.

Years into the future Senator Walter George, a Democrat, was proud of how states like his beloved Georgia were able to legally disenfranchise millions of voters. "Why apologize or evade?" he asked. "We have been very careful to obey the letter of the Federal Constitution—but we have been very diligent in violating the spirit of such amendments and such statutes as would have a Negro to believe himself the equal of a white man."

From 1873, with the *Slaughterhouse Cases*, and going forward with *Cruikshank*, *Plessy*, *Williams*, and other cases, the US Supreme Court systematically dismantled the Thirteenth, Fourteenth, and Fifteenth Amendments and rendered the Enforcement Acts dead letters. For strict constructionists, the court willfully ignored congressional intent and the history behind the laws and amendments.

At the onset of the twentieth century, in *Giles v. Harris* (1903), Justice Oliver Wendell Holmes wrote the majority opinion that federal courts couldn't rule to correct statewide injustices, even if they were committed by the state or its agent.

The US Supreme Court thus identified states as the ultimate defenders of rights, although Southern states had repeatedly proved themselves the ultimate violators of black peoples' rights. Through antiseptic, clinical, measured language, the highest court in the land entrusted the protection of life, liberty, and the pursuit of happiness for black Americans to the very same states that bragged this is "a white man's government."

So while the United States may have won the Civil War, and black people may have tasted freedom, the white opposition that ruled from the White House and the US Supreme Court all the way down through every statehouse in the South meant that real change was infinitesimal at best.

The *Chicago Defender* was one of the most powerful sources of encouragement for black people to leave the South during the Great Migration. Founder Robert S. Abbott is pictured at right. Editorials, poetry, and job listings all entreated black Southerners to move north and make the most of the new opportunities there. White Southern elitists then targeted the newspaper's distribution, attempting to limit the spread of its message.

DERAILING THE GREAT MIGRATION

IT WAS 1918. THE UNITED STATES WAS IN THE midst of a global war to make the world "safe for democracy," alleged President Woodrow Wilson. But during World War I it was anything but safe for black people in Georgia.

In south Georgia's Brooks County white planter Hampton Smith was notorious for his brutal treatment of black workers. His standard management practices included beatings, whippings, and the denial of wages. Not surprisingly, Smith had a hard time getting people to work on his plantation, the Old Joyce Place.

With fields to plow and a crop to harvest, he turned to an old, trusty labor supply: the local jail. Drawing on the peonage system, also known as debt slavery, set up after the Civil War, Smith routinely paid black people's fines, got them out of jail, then "hired" them until their debt was paid.

At least that was how it was supposed to work.

Smith ruthlessly worked people far past the point of any debt payoff and refused to pay them for their additional work. If challenged, he pulled out his whip. In May 1918, Smith abused the wrong black man: Sidney Johnson.

Following a dispute over work, Smith gave Johnson an unforgettable and unforgivable thrashing. Within a week, and after conspiring with several others on ending Smith's days, on Thursday night, May 16, 1918, Sidney Johnson shot Hampton Smith dead through a window of his home as he and Mrs. Smith ate supper. Smith died instantly. His wife, shot after she fled the house, survived her injury.

White retribution was swift, indiscriminate, and merciless.

In what the black-owned *Philadelphia Tribune* called a "five days lynching orgy," at least eleven blacks, most of whom had absolutely nothing to do with the shootings, were slaughtered. Perhaps none more gruesomely than Mary Turner, whose husband, Hayes, had been strung up from a tree on Saturday, May 18.

Having sent her two small children into hiding, the strong-willed and stubborn Mary, eight months pregnant, threatened that if she found out who murdered her husband she would seek to have them arrested.

Lynchers came for her the next day.

This mob included several of Hampton Smith's brothers, as well as a postal worker, an auditor for Standard Oil, and several farmers. In the woods near Folsom's Bridge, these white men dragged Mary Turner to a tree, stripped her naked, tied her ankles together, and strung her upside down. They then poured gasoline on her and set her on fire. The sight of the woman's stomach convulsing sent the men into a deeper frenzy. One took out a knife and sliced away at Mary's charred flesh until the fetus fell to the ground.

The baby uttered two cries.

Another man stepped forward and smashed the child's head into the red Georgia dirt with the heel of his boot.

Next, Turner's body was "riddled with bullets from high-powered rifles until it was no longer possible to recognize it as the body of a human being," wrote Walter White in a July 1918 memorandum to Georgia's governor Hugh Dorsey. Walter White was the assistant secretary of the National Association for the Advancement of Colored People (NAACP), an interracial civil rights organization founded in 1909.

In one form or another, what happened in Brooks County in the spring of 1918 was repeated over and over again throughout the South, with no arrests, trials, convictions, or prison sentences for the killers of black people. By 1920 there had been more than a thousand lynchings—that is, mob murders—per decade. In the former Confederate states almost 90 percent of the people lynched were black. Five states—Mississippi, Georgia, Texas, Alabama, and Louisiana—accounted for more than half of all lynchings in the nation.

One of the most macabre formats for these murders was spectacle lynching. Here a lynching was advertised in advance. Special promotional trains brought audience members, including women and children, to the slaughter because these gruesome events were standard family entertainment. Victims' severed body parts became souvenirs and decorations hung proudly in homes.

The terrors and horrors, however, did not always include physical death. Black women were particularly vulnerable to systematic sexual violence, because the rape of black women had long been part of a rite of passage for many white men. The widespread violence—lethal and otherwise—had pushed many blacks to reach the breaking point.

Within two months of the lynching of Mary Turner, at least five hundred black people left south Georgia and headed North. They joined hundreds, thousands of single people and families "willing to run any risk to get where they might breathe freer," as a black man reported of a group of about eight hundred Louisianians bound for Chicago back in 1917.

This was in the early days of the first phase of the Great Migration (1915–40), spurred initially by Northern industries' desperate need for labor. World War I, which began in the summer of 1914 and would not end until November 11, 1918, had drastically increased orders for manufactured goods such as guns, battleships, and steel. The war simultaneously reduced the traditional workforce of European immigrants responsible for producing those goods. The flow of immigrants dropped from more than 1.2 million in 1914 to just over 300,000 in 1915.

Looking for an untapped source of labor, business leaders soon hit upon the vast pool of black people previously shut out of the industrial workforce. Corporations such as the Pennsylvania Railroad Company hired labor agents to go below the

Mason-Dixon Line and convince black people to abandon Dixie and come north. For blacks, this was a chance to escape what W. E. B. Du Bois, editor of the NAACP's *Crisis* magazine, called a "Hell."

Forbidden, stifled ambition was part of this Hell.

"Whenever the colored man prospered too fast in this country, they worked every figure to cut you down, cut your britches off you," observed Ned Cobb, a black farmer and former sharecropper from Tallapoosa County, Alabama.

Similarly, an Alpharetta, Georgia, farmer explained that the South was no place for an honest, hardworking, ambitious man. "Better not accumulate much," he warned, because "no matter how hard and honest you work for it, as they—well, you can't enjoy it." In that stammer lay the bone-chilling truth that signs of prosperity could attract night riders and the bloodletting, torture, and land seizure that inevitably followed.

Equally vicious was the practice of "whitecapping," which today we'd call ethnic cleansing. In several Georgia and Mississippi counties, where plantations did not dominate the economy, local whites maimed, murdered, and terrorized blacks and, as the persecuted fled, seized all the land until one could "ride for miles and not see a black face."

The sharecropping system in which people rented and worked plots of land and gave landowners a share of their crops at year's end was yet another part of this Hell. Fewer than 20 percent of all sharecroppers ever made a profit at the end of the year, with the rest consigned to an ever-widening cavern of debt slavery. The system required sharecroppers to purchase all their supplies and foodstuffs from the landowner. At the end of the year, the accrued "debts" were deducted from the farmer's earnings. It was a system designed for abuse.

More often than not, landowners rigged the accounting. They charged inflated prices for goods—sometimes for items a sharecropper never even purchased. Most sharecroppers, therefore, never saw a penny. Instead, they owed their employer money at the start of a new year. Those who made a profit earned only between nine and forty-eight cents a day for a year's hard labor in the fields, or between $30 and $150 a year. And this was in the 1930s.

A challenge to the system, questioning the landowner's year-end accounting, could easily result in a lynching, spectacle or otherwise.

Paltry schooling in ramshackle hovels was also part of the Hell. In one Mississippi county, for example, 350 black children had only three teachers among them. The low priority Southern states placed on schools for black children was reflected in the meager funding and in the truncated school year. The school term for black children in Dawson County, Georgia, for example, was six weeks.

Added to this, black voter suppression remained rampant in the South.

As was the violence.

The vast majority of black people in the South had virtually no protection from a system that came painfully close to chattel slavery.

In their quest to "breathe freer"—a quest for better jobs,

housing, schools, and freedom from terror—black men and women collected what pennies they had to buy train tickets out of the South. They accepted free railroad passes from labor agents. They waited anxiously for fare sent from relatives who had already made it North.

When ready to shake the Southern dust from their feet, people hid their Sunday best beneath their work clothes so as not to tip off their employers that they were leaving. They abandoned their tools in the fields and left behind wages due to avoid alerting their bosses to their escape plans. They hitched rides on freight trains.

Migration is the story of America. It is foundational. From Pilgrims fleeing oppression in Europe in the 1600s and the millions of Americans going West after passage of the 1862 Homestead Act to the erection of the Statue of Liberty in New York's harbor (dedicated in 1886) and beyond. The movement of people fleeing tyranny, violence, and withered opportunities is precious, sacrosanct to Americans. "Freedom of movement" is a treasured American right.

Yet when thousands of black people began leaving the land below the Mason-Dixon Line, which along with the Ohio River became the dividing line between the North and the South, white Southern elites raged with cool, calculated efficiency.

These were mayors, governors, legislators, business leaders, and police chiefs. In the wood-paneled rooms of city halls, in the chambers of city councils, in the marbled state legislatures, and in sheriffs' offices, white government officials, working hand in hand with plantation, lumber mill, and mine owners, devised an array of ways to stop black people from exercising their right to freedom of movement.

Why?

Black labor was the foundation of the region's economy. Black people were also indispensable to the South's social and political structure.

Chattel slavery had marked blacks at the bottom— economically, politically, socially, culturally, physically, and intel- lectually. The base. If large numbers of black people left the South, then its entire socioeconomic structure, which was depen- dent on the support of that base, was in danger of collapsing. For white Southerners, black migration—black advancement and independence—was a threat to their culture along with their economy.

"Vigorous protests are going up from Georgia and Florida," reported the New Orleans *Times-Picayune* in August 1916, "espe- cially from Savannah and Jacksonville, against the work of the labor agents from the North, who are luring negro labor from the South Atlantic states to the great injury of employers in that section." The *Times-Picayune*, one of the South's most influential newspapers, continued: "There have been complaints on this score for some time, but the drain has, of late, become so great as to call for action."

Soon the South was blanketed with statutes to keep black people in their place, to stop them from controlling their own destinies.

Macon, Georgia, charged $25,000 for a license to recruit labor, a fee the equivalent of $2.76 million in 2016. What's more, to operate, a labor agent needed forty-five pillars of the white community to vouch for him.

How likely was that?

The city council in Jacksonville, Florida, required a labor agent to pay a thousand dollars for a recruiting license. Anyone who recruited the town's black workers without a license could face a six-hundred-dollar fine and sixty days in jail.

License or no license, labor agents lived with the threat of violence. Reverend D. W. Johnson, a black labor agent in Mississippi for the Mobile and Ohio Railroad, barely escaped detection for handing out free railroad passes to his people. One day, around twelve o'clock, two big, red-faced white men burst in with a bullwhip on their shoulders "and a rope and a gun in each of their hands." The white men vowed to kill anyone found with a pass. "Well, so they searched us one by one. . . . Had they pulled off my shoe, that'd been it for me. . . . Yeah, it was in the toe of my shoe."

Along with labor agents, the South's white elite had the *Chicago Defender* in its sights. Founded in 1905 by Robert Sengstacke Abbott, a native of St. Simons, Georgia, the *Defender* was the nation's most unapologetic, viscerally anti-South black newspaper. And it was central to the Great Migration.

The *Chicago Defender* was a primary channel of information about opportunities up north. Using a far-flung distribution system of black railroad porters, this weekly newspaper extended its influence well beyond Chicago and deep into the Mississippi Delta. The *Defender*'s stridency, its unrelenting embrace of blackness, and its open contempt for white racist regimes turned a simple newspaper into a symbol of black pride and defiance. Though its circulation figures may have been in the hundreds of thousands, the *Defender*'s impact was even greater: illiterate and barely literate people listened intently as the newspaper was read aloud in churches, diners, shacks, and barbershops.

Abbott's newspaper warned its readers not to be duped by entreaties from so-called black leaders that Dixie was their natural home. Those so-called black leaders included Robert Russa Moton.

After Booker T. Washington died in 1915, Moton became principal of Washington's vocational and teacher-training school in Tuskegee, Alabama: Tuskegee Institute (now University). Moton continued to preach the Wizard of Tuskegee's gospel. Washington, who became the unofficial president of black America after Frederick Douglass's demise in 1895, had urged blacks to accommodate Jim Crow—to forgo agitation for civil and political rights. Blacks best focus on honing skills, saving money, and acquiring property, said Washington. He argued that this was the way blacks needed to prove themselves worthy of rights.

Over and over again, the *Defender* instead pounded on the idea that Dixie needed to prove that it deserved black people. What the region's governments and employers had delivered so far left but one option, argued the *Defender*: "Get out of the South."

"You see they are not lifting their laws to help you, are they?" said the *Defender* of the Southern states. "Have they stopped their Jim Crow cars? . . . Will they give you a square deal in court yet? When a girl is sent to prison, she becomes the mistress of the guards and others in authority, and [black] women prisoners are put on the street to work, something they don't do to a white woman."

In encouraging migration, Abbott's newspaper published ad after ad about job opportunities in the North with wages that were unheard of in the South. The *Defender* also prominently displayed information about the availability of the National Urban League, a civil rights organization founded in 1910, to smooth peoples' transition from the rural South to the urban North.

Pictures of northern schools, homes, and lush public spaces that held out the promise of all that was possible were also ever-present in the pages of the *Chicago Defender*.

Determined to silence the *Defender*, Southern elites said to heck with the First Amendment's protection of freedom of speech and freedom of the press. The police chief in Meridian, Mississippi, had the *Defender* confiscated from dealers. Montgomery, Alabama, passed an ordinance that carried a penalty of up to six months' hard labor and a fine of one hundred dollars—or both—for writing, producing, or disseminating anything designed to entice laborers to leave the city for work elsewhere. A judge in Pine Bluff, Arkansas, saw to it that the distribution of the *Defender* anywhere in Jefferson County was prohibited.

These maneuvers succeeded only in forcing the newspaper underground. Like a resistance movement in a totalitarian society, a network of black railroad porters, ministers, and teachers, even under the stress of surveillance, circumvented the bans by using the postal system and smuggling the *Defender* in bulk goods. Indeed, the attempt to keep the newspaper out of black hands only increased its credibility and importance.

Southern states' assault on the First Amendment extended far beyond the *Defender*. In Georgia two men who carried a poem castigating the sharecropping system, lynching, and unequal pay were arrested, convicted, and sentenced to thirty days in jail for carrying incendiary literature. In Franklin, Mississippi, a black preacher was hit with a four-hundred-dollar fine and sentenced to five months on the county farm for selling the NAACP's *Crisis* magazine.

Despite the efforts of Southern officials to keep blacks in their place, wave after wave continued to leave. Nothing seemed to stop the flow. So the officials targeted the railroad system. The logic was simple: If the ideas that led to the exodus couldn't be stopped, then certainly the physical means by which hundreds of thousands had already left the region could be. A variety of tactics were employed. One was to physically prevent the trains from moving.

A waylaid train could wreak havoc with schedules even under optimal conditions, but conditions weren't optimal. With World War I raging, the shipment of personnel and matériel was crucial to supporting the Allies. Nevertheless, white Southern leaders put their need to stop the black migration above everything else.

It was most egregious in Mississippi. There, in Greenville, Greenwood, and Brookhaven, trains were stopped and sometimes sidetracked for days. The federal government finally stepped in when the police chief in Meridian, Mississippi, held up a train on a technicality. A US Marshal arrested the man on the spot.

In desperation, the mayor of New Orleans wired the president of the Illinois Central Railroad, asking his company to deny black people passage North. The reply was a primer on basic federal law and economics. The railroad executive explained that neither his company nor any other one, given the interstate commerce clause, could refuse to sell tickets or provide transport to paying customers. He also pointed out that, given the relatively high wages that blacks were now earning in the North, the South needed to brace itself. The exodus would surely continue.

In addition to interfering with interstate commerce, authorities went after would-be black passengers directly. In Albany, Georgia, the police ripped up the tickets of black passengers who were on the platform waiting to board a train. Memphis police inspector Earl Barnard seized twenty-six northbound blacks, charged them with vagrancy, then routed them to slave away on a plantation in Arkansas. In Hattiesburg, Mississippi, the ticket agent, under the advice and counsel of the town's citizens, simply refused to sell any tickets to black people. When they tried to circumvent the dragnet by walking many miles to use another station, the police manhandled them, then charged them with vagrancy.

"We are not slaveholders," wrote a resident of Dry Branch, Georgia, named Mack in a letter to the editor of the *Macon Daily Telegraph*, "we do not own the negroes; we cannot compel them to stay here."

Despite the white rage, despite the obstacles and roadblocks, black people continued to quit Dixie. All told, between 1915 and 1940, the Great Migration moved nearly 10 percent of the black population—1.5 million men and women, girls and boys—out of the South.

The NAACP recognized that the Sweets' case had pivotal importance in ensuring the safety of black people in their own homes, and the organization defended the family vigorously. Henry Sweet (left) with his legal team appointed by the NAACP, which included Julian Perry (second from left), Thomas Chawke (second from right), and Clarence Darrow (right).

THE SWEET ORDEAL

"MORE THOUSANDS KISS THE SOUTH A LAST GOOD-BY." So crowed the *Chicago Defender* on December 30, 1922.

But the land above the Mason-Dixon Line was no haven from oppression. Blacks who went north stepped into a new articulation of the seething, corrosive hatred underlying so much of the nation's social compact.

Beginning in 1917 and going into the 1920s, white-on-black riots erupted in cities around the nation. Whites went hunting for blacks to pummel, burn, and torture. In some instances blacks fought back. In all instances, they were outnumbered.

In the summer and fall of 1919, the rampages flamed in more than two dozen cities, including Chicago and Washington, DC. In Chicago alone, twenty-three blacks and fifteen whites were killed, and more than five hundred people were injured. One thousand black families were left homeless because their homes had been destroyed.

Because the bloodiest days occurred during the summer months, NAACP field secretary James Weldon Johnson, author of the national black anthem, "Lift Every Voice and Sing," named this awful period "Red Summer."

This white violence stemmed from the fact that, with World War I over and with so many soldiers mustered out, there was intense job competition in the States. Anxieties about housing also played a big role. Take for example Detroit, in Wayne County, Michigan, a city that once had a relatively small black population.

During the Great Migration that population grew and grew as the automobile industry provided job opportunities and possibilities for advancement almost unimaginable to black Southerners.

In 1914 the Ford Motor Company instituted an industry-setting pay scale of five dollars a day. Employees could make *in a single week* what it took a fortunate sharecropper two months—or more—to earn.

And so they kept coming.

By the mid-1920s, there were ten times as many blacks in the Motor City as there had been in 1915.

As Detroit's black population grew, the area where that community was supposed to live, a small stretch of land on the city's east side called Black Bottom, never expanded. Realtors, insurance agents, banks, and landlords devised a witches' brew of schemes to keep blacks hemmed in. Whites engaged in redlining (the denial of mortgages and other financial services). There were also restrictive covenants (agreements by property owners not to sell or rent to certain people). Such machinations locked out black people from wide swaths of Detroit's housing stock.

What was available to blacks in that crumbling, densely packed corner of the city was in horrible condition. Less than half the homes in Black Bottom had indoor plumbing, although in the urban north a bathroom was the norm. More than 15 percent of families were forced to live in one-room apartments. Nearly one-third of all black families were crammed into four-room homes.

Tired of cramped living conditions and fed up with rents way too high for ramshackle housing, black professionals sought to move out of Black Bottom. Dr. Ossian Sweet, who had emerged from abject poverty in the Deep South (Florida), was one such striver.

Dr. Ossian Sweet, a graduate of Howard University's medical school, had a thriving practice and was also on staff at Detroit's first hospital for blacks, Dunbar. He was husband to a beautiful, sophisticated woman, Gladys, and loving father to a baby girl, Marguerite, nicknamed Iva. With his carefully trimmed hair, tailored suits, and tortoiseshell glasses, Dr. Sweet was the embodiment of the American dream.

On September 8, 1925, this twenty-nine-year-old man began to move into his new home on the corner of Garland and Charlevoix. It was a nice bungalow—perhaps the finest house in the neighborhood. But this was no upscale community. Its white residents were not college educated. There wasn't a doctor, a lawyer, or an accountant among them. These whites were, for the most part, blue-collar workers, pipe fitters, factory foremen, and such.

But, as far as they were concerned, Dr. Sweet wasn't good enough to live in their neighborhood.

The day after the Sweets began moving into their home on Garland and Charlevoix, a mob formed outside of it. Having anticipated trouble, Sweet had asked some friends and relatives to be on hand. The men who agreed included his brother Otis, a dentist a few years younger than Ossian; and their younger brother, Henry, a student at Wilberforce University, a historically black school in Xenia, Ohio. William Davis, pharmacist and federal narcotics agent, had also signed on to help protect the Sweets and their property.

Dr. Ossian Sweet knew firsthand what a mob could do. For one, he had been in Washington, DC, during Red Summer when police allowed whites to rampage for several days slaughtering black people. The tide turned only after black World War I veterans had seen enough, polished their rifles, and began shooting.

There was another warning sign, too. About a month before the Sweets began moving into their home, Dunbar Hospital's cofounder and head of surgery, Dr. Alexander Turner, had tried to move into a home in an all-white part of Detroit: Tireman. That house quickly came under attack as a mob a thousand strong moved in to drive Dr. Turner and his family out. With police officers watching, at gunpoint Dr. Turner signed the deed to his house over to a neighborhood association.

Dr. Ossian Sweet was determined that this would not happen to him. Along with asking relatives and friends to be on hand, he had packed a small arsenal of guns and four hundred rounds of ammunition.

Sweet made sure to alert the police that trouble was brewing. Several officers showed up, but they hung back, even as the crowd grew.

The sun was setting when Otis Sweet and William Davis arrived in a taxi. Just then rocks began to pummel Ossian and Gladys's home.

Racial epithets singed the air.

As Otis and William rushed into the house, the mob was like a tsunami. "It looked like a human sea," Sweet later recalled. "Stones kept coming faster."

Henry Sweet and other men in the house grabbed guns. As rocks continued to rain down, they fired a full volley, twenty rounds. Two white men went down. One was Eric Houghberg, a twenty-two-year-old plumber, who would survive a leg wound. The other was Leon Breiner, a foreman at an auto plant. Breiner died on the spot from the bullet that ripped through his back.

Before long, the police sprang into action. They stormed the house and arrested Ossian, Gladys, and the nine men who had come to their aid.

The neighborhood had been primed for violence. After Dr. Sweet purchased his house, notices for a never-before-heard-of home-owners' association sprang up in the neighborhood. It invited all concerned residents to a meeting to determine how to stop the Sweets' "invasion." This meeting was held on the night of July 14, 1925.

The main speaker was from Tireman's homeowners' association, which had rid its neighborhood of the Turners and two other black families. We have the model for how to do this, this man told the throng of seven hundred. He rallied the crowd to rid their neighborhood of black people.

Thus, on September 9, 1925, a mob, which the media and the police initially estimated to be anywhere between three hundred and five thousand people, encircled the Sweets' home.

The clearly violent intent of the mob should have saved the Sweets from legal trouble. But Dr. Sweet's aspirations, his ambition, justified that intent in the minds of many white people in authority. In their eyes, his actions hadn't been a case of self-defense but of premeditated murder.

Inspector Norton Schuknecht, the police officer in charge at the Sweets' home on the night of the attack, maintained that there had been no crowd around the Sweets' house. There had been people milling about, he claimed, chatting with each other, but nothing to suggest a mob. In his estimation, Sweet and company had simply pointed its arsenal, taken aim, and fired at neighborly whites out for an evening stroll.

As for the rocks found in the upstairs bedroom amid so much broken glass, Schuknecht insisted that the stones came *after* the shooting. His sequence of events—shots, then rocks—voided the claim of self-defense.

This was the story Schuknecht repeated to the press, to the prosecutor, and eventually to a jury. He never let on about the impressions of his brother-in-law Otto Lemhagen, who was also on the scene that evening. Lemhagen "caught snatches of bitterness seething through the growing crowd," wrote Kevin Boyle in *Arc of Justice.*

A reporter from the *Detroit Free Press* who trudged through the rocks and debris at the Sweets' home listened to Schuknecht repeat the tale of neighbors walking the streets on a warm summer evening. The police officer also told reporters about Sweet's arsenal, implying that the house was a sniper's nest from which bullets were sprayed into a peaceful, calm neighborhood, killing a husband and father, while sending another man to the hospital. The *Detroit Free Press* ran with Schuknecht's explosive story. So did its rival, the *Detroit Times*.

Like Schuknecht, Philip Adler, a reporter for a third newspaper in town, the *Detroit News*, had also witnessed the attack on the Sweets' home. As Adler worked his way through the throng, he saw the rocks rain down on the house. Then he heard the shots—rocks, then shots. But Adler's editor refused to run his story. The *Detroit News* went with Schuknecht's account instead. By the next evening, Detroit's three newspapers had five hundred thousand copies blanketing the city, each condemning the Sweets as cold-blooded killers. Breiner's wife, already ill for many months, was believed to be "near death from shock," reported the *Detroit Times*, "though she has not been told that her husband's wound was fatal."

It was like throwing gasoline on a fire. Since World War I, Detroit had become Klan country, thirty-five thousand members strong. Only a coalition of white ethnics and blacks—arrayed around the slogan "Keep Detroit an American City!"—had managed to beat back the Klan's challenge for the mayor's office. Mayor Johnny Smith had helped weld that coalition, and blacks had come to view him as an ally. However, in the wake of the incident on Garland and Charlevoix, Mayor Smith sucker punched his black constituency in an open letter to the police commissioner on September 12.

Smith saw the KKK's hand behind the incident on Garland Avenue, but it wasn't the mob that incurred his wrath. It was the Sweets.

The Klan, Mayor Smith railed, had worked overtime to "induce Negroes to go into districts populated entirely by persons who would . . . resent such an invasion." He asserted that the point was to spark a race war that would blow Detroit apart and deliver the city to the KKK. Unfortunately, the mayor continued, the Ossian Sweets of this world had been willing pawns in this power play. If the black man would just stay in his place, he wrote, and quit demanding to exercise every last little right, then there would be peace in Detroit.

"I shall go further," Smith added. "I believe that any colored person who endangers life and property, simply to gratify his personal pride, is an enemy of his race as well as an incitant of riot and murder." For Detroit's liberal mayor, peace was based on black people quietly and gracefully accepting the fact that they had no right to their rights.

It was also on September 12, 1925, that Ossian, Gladys, and the others were charged with first degree murder and assault with intent to kill.

As he read the police reports, the interrogation transcripts, and the newspaper accounts of what happened on Garland Avenue, Wayne County prosecutor Robert Toms spotted an obvious weakness in his case: the arrestees, despite the fact that their stories rippled with inconsistencies, agreed that a bloodthirsty mob had descended upon the Sweet home and thrown rock after rock after rock. By any measure, that established self-defense. But Toms remained determined to bring Dr. Sweet, his wife, his brothers, and the others to trial.

Toms had his assistant prosecutor, Edward Kennedy, conduct additional interviews with the police and neighbors to shore up the case against Ossian Sweet and company. Two key points needed to be nailed down: the size of the crowd and the time when the rocks were first thrown.

Michigan law defined a mob as more than twelve armed people, or thirty unarmed, gathered intent on intimidating or harming a party that resulted in twenty-five dollars or more in property damage. And remember: it wasn't just the Sweets who had insisted that there was a mob; the very newspapers that had branded them killers described hundreds of people swarming Garland Avenue.

Schuknecht's version, though, had to be supported, and Kennedy's job was to nail down the police inspector's story and then get independent corroborating testimony.

When Kennedy interviewed the inspector the day after the riot in the Sweets' home, he asked, "Did you observe any people standing in front of the house, directly across from the Sweets?"

Schuknecht replied in the affirmative.

"How many would you say there were?"

"I would say twelve or fifteen people across the street there."

The assistant prosecutor strongly suspected that Schuknecht's answers were rehearsed, informed not by the truth but by a quick glance at Michigan law books. That was a problem, but it was not insurmountable.

As he turned to the next-door neighbors, the tone of his questions, along with his body language, helped steer them to the right answers.

These corroborating statements buttressing police evidence convinced prosecutor Toms to proceed. He would as well, wrote the author of *Arc of Justice,* ensure that "the Sweets would face an all-white jury . . . and if he couldn't convince twelve Caucasians to convict eleven Negroes who invaded a white neighborhood armed to the teeth," well, then he "didn't deserve his salary." Toms had already convinced the judge to deny the defendants bail. He wanted them to languish in jail until the jury decided their fate months later.

There was, however, a moment of mercy. After spending several weeks in jail, on October 5, 1925, Gladys Sweet was released on a five-thousand-dollar bail. One can only imagine this woman's emotions when reunited with her little girl, Iva. That reunion would prove to be bittersweet.

The trial of *The People v. Ossian Sweet, Gladys Sweet, et al.* began on November 5, 1925. Early on, Toms painted a picture of the Sweets' barely furnished house with a stockpile of weapons and ammunition.

He made clear that all those guns and bullets and very little furniture were the telltale signs that the defendants had moved into the house on Garland to commit murder. They had no intention of setting up a home. Toms told the jury that this was evident from the results of the interrogations.

Weeks earlier, at the police station, Edward Kennedy had

kept after Dr. Sweet about the guns: When had they arrived? Why were weapons in the house? Who had brought them? Sweet dodged and dodged, but the assistant prosecutor was relentless.

"When you moved in, you had the arsenal up there with you . . . knowing you were going to have trouble, didn't you?"

"Yes," the doctor finally said.

If Sweet knew there was going to be trouble, Kennedy probed, "Why did you move in there, then?"

Sweet's response, "Because I bought the house . . . and I felt I had a right to live in it," carried no weight.

Henry Sweet eventually admitted that he had fired a rifle, but only after the rocks "began coming in on me." His claim of self-defense was as irrelevant as his brother's against the unfolding portrait of murderous conspirators holed up in the house on Garland.

Weeks later, Kennedy's boss summed up his case at the end of the trial: the invasion of a white neighborhood, the arsenal in a sparsely furnished house, the admission that shots had rung out from the upstairs window—it all meant only one thing: Leon Breiner was "shot through the back, from ambush," Toms told the jury, "and you can't make anything out of those facts . . . but cold-blooded murder."

"The importance of the case to the Negro cause was obvious," wrote the NAACP's Walter White years later. "If the Sweets were not given adequate legal defense, if the ancient Anglo-Saxon principle that 'a man's home is his castle' were not made applicable to Negroes as well as to others, we knew that other and even more determined attacks would be made upon the homes of Negroes throughout the country."

The NAACP had rushed to pull together a legal team for the defendants. This team included the high-profile trial attorney Clarence Darrow. In 1924 Darrow had defended two young white men of Chicago, Nathan Leopold and Richard Loeb, who had kidnapped and murdered a fourteen-year-old white boy just for the thrill of it. With Darrow as their attorney, Leopold and Loeb were spared the death penalty and instead got life in prison plus ninety-nine years. A few months before the Sweets moved into their home, the *State of Tennessee v. John Thomas Scopes*, known as the Scopes Monkey Trial, ended. Here Darrow defended John Thomas Scopes, a high school teacher in Dayton, Tennessee, arrested for teaching evolution in a public school, which was against Tennessee law.

In *The People v. Ossian Sweet, Gladys Sweet, et al.*, patiently and meticulously, Darrow and his co-counsel, Arthur Garfield Hays, picked apart the lies, the coached testimony, and the half-truths of the neighbors, homeowners' association leaders, and police. The size of the crowd inched well above Schuknecht's twelve or fifteen. The rocks were acknowledged as a hailstorm. Also, eventually a homeowners' association discussion concerning property values was revealed to have been about the level of violence necessary to oust the Sweets.

During closing arguments, Darrow stressed that the prosecution's case was based on racism and lies. What's more, he added, the prosecution's witnesses had "perjured themselves on behalf of what they think is their noble, Nordic race."

"Acquit my clients," Darrow insisted, "and repair the damage caused by America's shameful original sin." The case went to the jury on November 25, 1925, the day before Thanksgiving.

After the jury's forty-six-hour deliberation, Darrow did not get what he wanted—but neither did prosecutor Toms.

Five jurors voted for acquittal. Seven, however, repeatedly voted to convict Ossian and Henry Sweet for murder.

The result: a hung jury.

The presiding judge, Frank Murphy, declared a mistrial.

Toms refused to drop the charges. He was pledged to retry all the defendants, only this time it would be one by one. First up, Henry Sweet. His trial began on April 19, 1926.

Darrow was more than ready. This time he suspected that the lying would be all the more obvious, with, as James Weldon Johnson recalled, "many of the prosecution witnesses [having] forgotten the testimony they gave at the first trial." Even the press, taking notice of these irregularities, had begun to tone down its attacks on the defendants.

Having already established that there had been so many cars in the area on the night of September 9, 1925, that the police had had to barricade the street, Darrow said to the jury, "There is nothing but prejudice in this case. If it was reversed, and eleven white men had shot and killed a black while protecting their home and their lives against a mob of blacks, nobody would have dreamed of having them indicted. . . . They would have been given medals instead."

With each crack in the witnesses' testimony, Toms's case fell apart. Still he plowed on, trying to convince the jury that the death of Leon Breiner, a white man, was all that mattered.

The jury didn't buy it. The foreman pronounced Henry Sweet "not guilty" on May 19, 1926. After Henry's acquittal, Robert Toms announced that he would not retry Ossian, Gladys, and the others, though he didn't officially drop the charges until the summer of 1927.

Tragedy loomed in the lives of the Sweets after their ordeal. Gladys, who had been cooking dinner when the rocks and bullets started flying, came down with tuberculosis, contracted, she believed, while she was held for nearly a month in the dank, crowded, and unsanitary Wayne County Jail. Daughter Iva also became infected. The two-year-old died a few months after Henry Sweet's trial, in August 1926. Two years later, in late November 1928, Gladys died of tuberculosis. Henry Sweet died of the same disease in 1940.

As for Ossian, he tried to soldier on, but he eventually faced foreclosure, sold the home on Garland and Charlevoix, and moved into a small apartment in Black Bottom.

On Saturday, March 19, 1960, Sweet put a gun to his head and pulled the trigger.

Robert Russa Moton High School in Prince Edward County, Virginia, was an early battleground for the school desegregation movement. Even though black students made up nearly half of the county's population, they were forbidden from attending the main school in town and instead placed in cheap tar-paper buildings with no heat or electricity. The students' lawsuit against the school district became one of the cases rolled into *Brown v. Board of Education*. Above, some of the students from the school, including Dorothy E. Davis (center with glasses).

10

BUILDING TOWARD *BROWN*

JIM CROW DOMINATED THE LIVES OF BLACK
people in America from 1890 well into the twentieth century.
From conception to coffin, there was no nook or cranny of a
black person's life that it did not touch.

In the 1930s the NAACP launched a campaign in the courts
to destroy Jim Crow—to overturn the 1896 *Plessy v. Ferguson* decision that ushered in government-sanctioned racial segregation in
America.

The brilliant Charles Hamilton Houston was the campaign's
mastermind. This member of Washington, DC's black elite was
a graduate of the city's all-black M Street school (now Dunbar
High), once one of the nation's premier high schools bar none.
Houston went on to earn his bachelor's degree (Phi Beta Kappa)
from Amherst College. After a stint in the segregated army during
World War I, he attended Harvard Law School, where he was its
first black editor of *Harvard Law Review* and where he earned a

bachelor of law degree in 1922 and a doctor of judicial science the next year. Thanks to a Sheldon Fellowship, Houston followed that up with an additional year of study of the law at the University of Madrid. After that, he joined his father's law firm in DC.

When Charles Hamilton Houston set his sights on killing Jim Crow, he used the *Plessy* decision itself as a weapon.

After the US Supreme Court first announced that 1896 decision, states seized on the "separate" aspect of the edict almost immediately, creating racially distinct facilities from telephone booths to cemeteries. For nearly six decades, the same states had consistently failed to provide anything approximating "equal" for America's black citizens. This was the Achilles' heel that NAACP lawyers attacked.

The association's initial thrust was at higher education. The NAACP insisted that states establish for black people public law schools and doctoral programs of the same caliber as the ones for white people. In response, white Southern leaders tried to parry the NAACP's challenge and still meet *Plessy*'s threshold.

Missouri, for example, opted to define "equal" as paying for black people to get their legal education in Nebraska or Iowa. In the case *Missouri ex rel. Gaines v. Canada* (1938), the US Supreme Court would have none of it. The justices ordered the University of Missouri to open its doors to black people.

The Lone Star State attempted to re-create the University of Texas at Austin's law school for black students in four rooms below street level in a run-down building on the grounds of the Texas State Capitol. As far as the court could tell, it failed miserably (*Sweatt v. Painter*, 1950).

The Sooner State hoped to keep *Plessy* intact by admitting blacks to the University of Oklahoma but putting them in separate spaces on campus. That hardly constituted "equal." In *McLaurin v. Oklahoma State Regents* (1950) the High Court ruled that those internal racial barriers were unconstitutional.

The NAACP made it painfully clear that if states wanted to keep Jim Crow on the throne they would have to pay dearly for it.

Already Jim Crow had cost America's black children dearly. Delaware had essentially abdicated all responsibility for the education of its youngest black citizens. Black communities did their best to stand in the gap. By 1910, they had built eighty-one schools. However, due to limited resources, these schools were no more than shacks without decent lighting, plumbing, or enough desks.

Delaware's white segregationists were not only opposed to *public* funding for black schools but also balked at *private* intervention, such as that of white industrialist and Delaware native Pierre S. du Pont. In the 1920s Du Pont built more than eighty schools in Delaware for black children, at a cost of about two hundred thousand dollars, but that work was often "delayed" to tamp down whites' antagonism.

Despite Du Pont's efforts, and those of black communities, things were still bad. Delaware had only one public high school for blacks, Howard, in Wilmington, founded in 1867 and, like so many other black schools, named after Oliver O. Howard, who had headed up the Freedmen's Bureau during Reconstruction.

Delaware's neglect of young black minds was devastating. By 1950, black adults in Delaware had finished, on average, only

7.2 years of school. In contrast, whites had finished more than 10 years. Only 505 black men and women in the entire state had earned a bachelor's degree. Not surprisingly, black income, which averaged a little more than a thousand dollars a year, was not even one-third of white income.

Virginia, the wealthiest Southern state and the fifth richest in the entire nation—and a state with a constitution and statutes requiring the provision of public schools and compulsory attendance—was equally determined not to educate its black population.

In Prince Edward County, for example, there was no black high school until 1939: Robert Russa Moton High in Farmville. It was built for 180 students, but by 1947 this school "was jammed with more than twice the number of students it was designed to hold," wrote Peter Irons in *Jim Crow's Children*. The student body had risen to nearly five hundred.

Blacks were 45 percent of the county's population.

Blacks paid taxes.

Yet . . .

To handle the overflow at Moton High, the all-white school board erected three tar-paper shacks. These shacks had neither insulation nor electricity. "Chicken coops was what people said they looked like," remembered former student John Stokes of those shacks heated with potbellied stoves. Stokes also remembered visitors taking pictures of the shacks "to show the people back home how backward we were."

The other black schools in Prince Edward County were also poorly constructed. As they had no indoor plumbing, students, like the staff, had to use outhouses. The fifteen facilities for 2,000 black students were valued at $330,000. In contrast, the seven brick schoolhouses for 1,400 white students had been appraised at $1.2 million. And those schools had indoor restrooms and modern furnaces.

In the Deep South, the educational opportunities were at least as bleak. The disparity in student-to-teacher ratios in mid-1930s Atlanta, for example, was staggering. For blacks, there were 82 students for every teacher. The ratio for whites was 35 to 1.

Overcrowded black schools led to significantly shortened school days as students rotated through in shifts. When public funding was finally increased, the disparities actually grew. In 1942, the Atlanta school board allocated $75 more in support per capita for white students than for black students. By 1946, that figure had climbed to almost $80. As Tomiko Brown-Nagin stated in her history of the civil rights movement in Atlanta, black students had to contend with "overcrowded classrooms, decrepit school buildings, inadequate numbers of textbooks, schools lacking libraries, cafeterias, gymnasiums." They also had to put up with double and triple sessions where "85 percent of all black elementary school students attended class for only half the day during the 1947–48 school year."

In Louisiana during the 1943–44 school year, similar funding disparities echoed throughout the school system. At the elementary level alone, for example, the East Baton Rouge parish spent $67.79 per capita on white children while doling out a mere third of that for each black student. East Feliciana Parish, thirty miles north of Baton Rouge, had a per capita allocation of $121.64 for whites in kindergarten through sixth grades and a paltry

$18.92 for each black child in those grades. Overall, Louisiana spent $76.34 on each white elementary school child and only $23.99 on each black one.

Separate and woefully unequal school systems produced sprawling, uneducated black populations. And this had devastating, long-term consequences. Millions of black people were stuck with the lowest-paying jobs—if any job. Low income translated into dilapidated housing, for example. And poor housing often led to subpar health.

By the mid-1940s, in Alabama, Georgia, Louisiana, South Carolina, and Mississippi, with a combined black population of 4.7 million, *more than half* of all black adults had less than five years of formal education. In South Carolina and Louisiana, *more than 60 percent* of black men and women had only gone to fourth or fifth grade.

In one court case after the next, from 1935 to 1950, the NAACP had convincingly demonstrated that southern governments were simply incapable of meeting *Plessy's* standard of "separate but equal." That left Dixie in grave judicial danger. And that was what Charles Hamilton Houston had aimed for. With the legal precedent duly laid in cases such as *McLaurin v. Oklahoma State Regents* and others mentioned earlier, the time had come to take down *Plessy* as fundamentally unconstitutional.

Houston died in 1950. His protégé, future US Supreme Court associate justice Thurgood Marshall, led the next phase of this legal battle. This native of Maryland had graduated cum laude from the historically black Lincoln University in Chester County, Pennsylvania. After the University of Maryland's law school denied Marshall admission because of his race, he enrolled in Howard University's law school, which Houston, as vice dean, had single-handedly transformed into a first-rate institution.

Starting in 1950, Thurgood Marshall and fellow NAACP lawyers amassed cases challenging the constitutionality of Jim Crow public schools, from Delaware, Virginia, South Carolina, Kansas, and Washington, DC.

The Virginia case (*Davis v. County School Board of Prince Edward County*) sprang from the strike Barbara Johns, John Stokes, and other teens at Robert Moton High launched in the spring of 1951 in protest of their shabby educational opportunities. The lead plaintiff in this case was one of the Moton High protestors, Dorothy E. Davis.

In the case in South Carolina (*Briggs v. Elliott*), Harry Briggs Sr., a World War II veteran who worked as gas station attendant, was among the twenty parents who brought a lawsuit against Clarendon County's school board president, R. W. Elliott. They brought their separate-and-unequal lawsuit after Elliott thumbed his nose at their request that the county provide school buses for their children just as it did for white children.

The Kansas case arose out of the plight of children in Topeka, among them Linda Brown. Linda and others were forced to travel great distances to attend school, because the ones in their neighborhoods were for white children only. Linda's father, Oliver Brown, a minister, was the lead plaintiff in this case: *Brown v. Topeka Board of Education*, commonly known as simply *Brown*.

In December 1952 Thurgood Marshall argued before the US Supreme Court that racial segregation violated the equal protection clause of the Fourteenth and, in the case from DC, the due process clause of the Fifth Amendment. (The equal protection clause only applies to states, not to federal territories.)

Hoping to get the NAACP to drop the lawsuits, Southern states had dangled a carrot: a series of school-equalization packages, that is, commitments to build schools for black children that were on par with those for white children. New black high schools suddenly popped up across the South. While these schools may have been improvements, they never truly made the grade as "equal" to schools for white youth.

St. Louis–born Roy Wilkins, the NAACP's executive secretary, its chief, scoffed at white Southern leaders' "scramble . . . to upgrade black school shanties in the vain hope of heading off pressure to do away with them entirely." The future was at stake here. Black people were determined to use every resource at their disposal to ensure that not one more generation fell into the abyss of illiteracy, poverty, and economic vulnerability.

"I offered my life for a decadent democracy, and I'm willing to die rather than let these children down," thundered Baptist minister L. Francis Griffin from the pulpit of his church in Farmville, Virginia. Known as the "Fighting Preacher," Griffin, who had served in the Jim Crow military during World War II, had been one of the firebrands behind the case in Prince Edward County and behind the blanket case, *Brown.*

Standing fast was no easy thing. People paid a price.

Teenage Barbara Johns, who was in the forefront of that student strike at Moton High in Prince Edward County, had to be spirited out of the state by her parents to go live with her uncle, the dynamic Reverend Vernon Johns, in Alabama.

Reverend Joseph DeLaine, one of the parents in the South Carolina case bundled into *Brown*, faced the unbridled wrath of local whites: "Before it was over, they fired him from the little schoolhouse at which he had taught devotedly for ten years," wrote Richard Kluger in his book *Simple Justice.* "And they fired his wife and two of his sisters and a niece." DeLaine was also threatened with violence, and "they sued him on trumped-up charges and convicted him in a kangaroo court." This was not the end of DeLaine's ordeal. Among other things, his house was torched. It burned "to the ground while the fire department stood around watching the flames consume the night."

And it wasn't just the activist types who stood fast. Once-reliable Negroes—people the power structure had always been able to count on to preach patience to black people—refused to lend their support to equalization schemes and had refused to urge the NAACP to withdraw *Brown* from the Supreme Court's docket.

The white response was emphatic.

Mississippi Democrat senator James O. Eastland vowed, "We will protect and maintain white supremacy throughout eternity." Mississippi governor Fielding Wright concurred, adding, "regardless of consequences."

Beating back a 1949 challenge from black parents to equalize the schools, in the fall of 1953 Georgia's governor Herman Talmadge had proposed a constitutional amendment that would authorize the state legislature to scrap the public-school system altogether and fund instead white children's tuition at private schools. "As long as I am Governor," Talmadge once vowed, "Negroes will not be admitted to white schools." While threatening to scuttle the public system, the governor never contemplated any educational alternatives for Georgia's more than three hundred thousand black children.

Similarly, Mississippi's legislature crafted a constitutional amendment to abolish public schools. In case that didn't pass, they also came up with pupil-placement legislation that would empower school officials to place certain students in certain schools. Not based on race, oh no, but on things like "ability" or a child not being "a good fit." A pupil-placement law would give school boards inordinate power to keep more than three hundred and twenty-five thousand black children from gaining access to better-resourced white schools.

In South Carolina, James F. Byrnes, who had been a congressman, a US senator, a US Supreme Court justice, and then secretary of state before becoming governor, supported a slew of legislative proposals—from selling public-school property to private individuals and pupil-placement laws to abolishing the public-school system. "Of only one thing can we be certain," Byrnes swore back in 1951. "South Carolina will not now, nor for some years to come, mix white and colored children in our schools." Similar reaction spread throughout the South and threatened to erupt more seriously in the event that the Supreme Court ruled *Plessy*, and therefore Jim Crow, unconstitutional.

In their battle against school integration, white segregationists had the sympathy of President Dwight D. Eisenhower, a native of Texas.

In the spring of 1954, shortly before the High Court was to rule on *Brown*, at the behest of his friend governor Byrnes, Eisenhower hosted a small dinner party at the White House. One of the guests was US Supreme Court chief justice Earl Warren. The president explained to Warren, a Californian, that Southerners "are not bad people. All they are concerned about is to see that their sweet little girls are not required to sit in school alongside big overgrown Negroes."

At the same time, the president warned Governor Byrnes that a last-ditch effort to put more money into black schools would be prohibitively expensive. During World War II, the federal government estimated that it would have taken $43 million dollars (equivalent to a little more than $1.3 trillion in 2016) to equalize the schools in America. Byrnes and others, however, believed the expense was worth it to keep Jim Crow the uncontested law of the land.

On Monday, May 17, 1954, in a unanimous decision, the US Supreme Court ruled on the five cases bundled into *Brown*. The verdict: Jim Crow schools were unconstitutional.

The significance of the High Court's judgment was not confined to education. "If segregation is unconstitutional in educational institutions, it is no less so unconstitutional in other aspects of our national life," observed Charles Johnson, president of Fisk University in Nashville, Tennessee.

Robert Jackson, a professor at another historically black school, Virginia Union University in Richmond, called the *Brown* decision "the most exciting moment." He added: "A lot of us haven't been breathing for the past nine months. But today the students reacted as if a heavy burden has been lifted from their shoulders. They see a new world opening up for them and those that follow them."

At that moment, it appeared that citizenship—true citizenship—might finally be at hand for blacks in America. It was

FROM THE US SUPREME COURT OPINION IN *BROWN*,
written by Chief Justice Earl Warren

In approaching this problem, we cannot turn the clock back to 1868, when the [Fourteenth] Amendment was adopted, or even to 1896, when *Plessy v. Ferguson* was written. We must consider public education in the light of its full development and its present place in American life throughout the Nation. Only in this way can it be determined if segregation in public schools deprives these plaintiffs of the equal protection of the laws.

Today, education is perhaps the most important function of state and local governments. Compulsory school attendance laws and the great expenditures for education both demonstrate our recognition of the importance of education to our democratic society. It is required in the performance of our most basic public responsibilities, even service in the armed forces. It is the very foundation of good citizenship. Today it is a principal instrument in awakening the child to cultural values, in preparing him for later professional training, and in helping him to adjust normally to his environment. In these days, it is doubtful that any child may reasonably be expected to succeed in life if he is denied the opportunity of an education. Such an opportunity, where the state has undertaken to provide it, is a right which must be made available to all on equal terms. . . .

We conclude that, in the field of public education, the doctrine of "separate but equal" has no place. Separate educational facilities are inherently unequal.

"the greatest victory for the Negro people since the Emancipation Proclamation," wrote the *New York Amsterdam News*, a Harlem-based weekly.

The NAACP's taciturn Wilkins could barely contain himself. "May 17, 1954, was one of life's sweetest days."

To Southern leaders who had already been readying their political arsenal, the *Brown* decision was but a declaration of war.

"My sense of euphoria that evening was a bit naïve," Wilkins later admitted looking back on May 17, 1954. "Swept away, elevated, exalted, I failed to anticipate the ferocity of the resistance that quickly grew up in the Deep South."

The Little Rock Nine, Thurgood Marshall, and civil rights activist Daisy Bates. After the Little Rock Nine integrated Central High School in Arkansas in 1957, Governor Orval Faubus shut down all of Little Rock's public high schools the following year.

BEATING DOWN *BROWN*

TRADITIONALLY, WHITE SOUTHERN RESISTANCE to the *Brown* decision has been captured by images of violence that followed the Supreme Court decision.

The angry mob of mostly white housewives hounding the traumatized fifteen-year-old Elizabeth Eckford on September 4, 1957: her first day of school at the once lily-white Central High in Little Rock, Arkansas.

The wreckage of Hattie Cotton Elementary School in Nashville, Tennessee, after it was bombed in wee hours of the morning of September 10, 1957. The day before, Patricia Watson had started first grade there as the school's first and only black student.

There's also the Norman Rockwell painting of a disturbing scene that features pigtailed six-year-old Ruby Bridges surrounded by towering National Guardsmen on November 14, 1960. They stride by tomato-splattered walls further disgraced with racial slurs and "KKK" as they make their way to New Orleans's William Frantz Elementary School, once all-white.

None of that violence would have happened, however, and certainly would not have received the broader societal stamp of approval, if the respected elements in white society—governors, legislators, US senators, congressmen, and even, more tepidly, the president of the United States—had not condoned defiance of and contempt for the US Supreme Court and the constitutional provision that its decisions are the law of the land.

In the North, where racial segregation was intense, the defiance was subtle but effective. In 1957, for example, Milwaukee's school board instituted "intact busing" that carried black children in overcrowded schools to white schools, kept them isolated in a separate classroom, and then ferried them back home again. The overt, even violent response to *Brown* did not occur in the North until much later, in the 1970s, most spectacularly in Boston.

On the other hand, the Southern states made clear that they were ready for war from the get-go. The first step was to ensure that only those who felt threatened by *Brown* could vote. As Numan V. Bartley revealed in *The Rise of Massive Resistance*, by 1944—ten years before *Brown*—only 5 percent of nearly five million, or roughly two hundred and fifty thousand blacks eligible to vote were registered in the states of the old Confederacy. That left millions politically voiceless.

As trying as it had been for blacks to register to vote before *Brown*, it became much more so after the ruling. Mississippi, for example, reinforced an amendment requiring superior literacy and an ability to interpret the state's constitution. Given that nearly 53 percent of Mississippi's black adults had fewer than five years of education, compared with only 10 percent of their white peers, the emphasis on literacy and interpretation of a complicated legal document, while appearing race-neutral, was, in fact, targeted directly at black Mississippians.

What's more, state authorities required blacks *already* registered to vote to reregister. These people faced the gauntlet of literacy tests, understanding clauses, and the whims of the registrar. That move alone caused the number of black registered voters in Mississippi, for example, to plummet by two-thirds. As late as 1960, more than 98 percent of black Mississippians eligible to vote were not registered to do so.

On May 31, 1955, the Supreme Court handed down an implementation decision, *Brown II.* The High Court said that desegregation in public schools must happen "with all deliberate speed."

Segregationists remained defiant.

Deep South states and Virginia added to their arsenals the discredited legal hocus pocus of interposition: a state's claim to the right to put itself between federal law and US citizens in order to stop enforcement of rulings with which the state disagreed.

State representative Sam Engelhardt declared that interposition would "serve notice on the rest of the nation that Alabama and the South will not accept integration."

South Carolina's new governor, George Bell Timmerman Jr., endorsed the unanimous legislative resolution that "condemns and protests against the illegal encroachment by the central government" on the state's sovereignty "and against the grave threat to the constitutional government implicit in the decisions of the

Supreme Court of the United States." Just as at Fort Sumter, where the Civil War started, the first shots were aimed at the federal government.

If Georgia's legislature had had its way, the Constitution's Thirteenth, Fourteenth, and Fifteenth Amendments would be repealed. It passed a resolution to petition the US Congress to do just this. The Georgia legislature also wanted the Supreme Court justices impeached. As if its rebelliousness wasn't evident enough, on July 1, 1956, the Peach State adopted a new flag, one designed by segregationist John Sammons Bell. A Confederate battle flag took up two-thirds of the new banner. This flag flew above the state capitol until 2001.

After *Brown*, White Citizens' Councils sprang up throughout the South. These groups were generally made up of middle-income and upper-income white folk. White Citizens' Councils had but one objective: destroy *Brown*.

The Texas White Citizens' Council issued the disclaimer "We do not advocate violence or any form of illegal activity." In its mission to prevent school desegregation it pledged to "do so by any means at [its] command which falls within the law." The Texas Council dared to propose an amendment to the US Constitution that would require the Supreme Court to answer to Congress.

Yes, they wanted to destroy the central concept of checks and balances in the Constitution.

Yes, at a time when Southern Democrats had a stranglehold on both houses of Congress, the Texas White Citizens' Council wanted to ensure that the Supreme Court would be at Dixie's beck and call.

After such opening salvos came the shot heard around America.

On March 12, 1956, Representative Howard Smith, a Democrat from Virginia, and Senator Walter George, a Democrat from Georgia, introduced the "Declaration of Constitutional Principles" before their respective chambers in Congress. This declaration, which became known as the Southern Manifesto, asserted that the Supreme Court had violated states' rights, abused judicial authority, and undercut the separation of powers. One hundred and one members of Congress, all from states of the old Confederacy, signed it. Senator Lyndon Johnson, Democrat from Texas, was among the handful of holdouts.

The Southern Manifesto signaled to the constituencies of its signers that Massive Resistance to *Brown* was not some base, primeval white supremacy but rather a principled, patriotic stand to defend the Constitution. The Southern Manifesto sanctioned the use of the levers of government to defy the US Supreme Court until, with the idea that the federal judiciary and black people would tire of the fight and *Brown* would simply collapse. The strategy's name was derived from US senator from Virginia Harry Flood Byrd's declaration to colleagues weeks before the Southern Manifesto was released: "If we can organize the Southern States for massive resistance to [the *Brown* decision]," said Byrd, "I think that, in time, the rest of the country will realize that racial integration is not going to be accepted in the South."

The game plan of *stall and defy* was now in place. Southern states used and abused the legal process to pass one unconstitutional law after the next. They knew that the process to overturn the statutes would be costly. But in the meantime, all the motions, hearings, affidavits, rulings, and appeals kept *Brown* at bay.

Those extended legal battles allowed year after year to drizzle. During that drip of time, separate and decidedly unequal schools continued. Black children continued to be consigned to some of the worst education. Proud of the consequences, one man bragged, "As long as we can legislate, we can segregate." Indeed, by 1963, not one black child had attended a white public school in South Carolina, Alabama, or Mississippi, for example.

Black parents stood up for their children, hauling states back into court. One of those states was Arkansas, where Elizabeth Eckford and eight other black teenagers—the "Little Rock Nine"—braved the task of integrating Little Rock's Central High in 1957. Black people were furious that rather than integrate, Governor Orval Faubus had shut down all Little Rock's high schools in 1958.

The subsequent US Supreme Court decision in *Cooper v. Aaron* was unequivocal: in Brown "the Court's interpretation of the Fourteenth Amendment was the supreme law of the land and had to be obeyed," wrote Charles J. Ogletree Jr. in *All Deliberate Speed: Reflections on the First Half-Century of Brown v. Board of Education.*

Like *Brown*, the *Cooper v. Aaron* ruling only baited white officials in the South. In an amazingly wrongheaded interpretation of the US Constitution, Arkansas argued that it was the state's *governor,* not the US Supreme Court, who had the right and power to determine the law of the land.

Governor Orval Faubus's Fort Sumter moment happened the minute that he closed the public high schools in Little Rock in 1958 and all the legislative machinery of privatization that had been previously holstered came out blazing. Between donations totaling more than $300,000, state funding of $176 per year per student, and taxpayer-subsidized busing to private academies, Little Rock had the means for most white children to remain in school while the state simultaneously defied the Supreme Court by keeping blacks locked out. While white children attended those private academies, "black children in Little Rock were without [high] school altogether," lamented Wilkins, the NAACP chief.

This lasted for a year and is known as the "Lost Year."

The situation went from bad to worse in Upper South states too. In Delaware a district court ruling authorized a *twelve-year* delay in implementing *Brown.*

In Virginia, when local school boards in Charlottesville, Norfolk, and Front Royal were under federal court orders to admit black students, Governor James Lindsay Almond closed, in his words, every "school threatened with desegregation" in those cities in September 1958. In doing so, Governor Almond not only hurt black children. He shut out nearly thirteen thousand white children from getting an education. "Pundits wasted no time," Jill Ogline Titus wrote in *Brown's Battleground,* "in laying full blame for education disruption at the feet of the 'NAACP agitators.'"

. . .

School closures spread to now-besieged Prince Edward County. Laws were passed to close the public schools, siphon tax dollars into private academies, and pay tuition for white students. Absolutely nothing was put in place for 2,700 black children. This would last for *five* years.

The defiance of Prince Edward County was singular—no other school system in the nation remained closed for five years (1959 to 1964) rather than comply with *Brown*.

Only a small number of black families were able to send their children to live with relatives in, say, Boston, Chicago, or New York City, and have them attend school there. Those children were lucky. As for the rest . . .

During those five long years, critical in terms of child development, most black children in Prince Edward County spent their formative education time in activity centers that the black community cobbled together. The Baltimore *Afro-American* reported that these makeshift centers, some in basements, some in churches, others in abandoned shacks, staffed overwhelmingly by housewives and those with only a high school diploma, could not provide anything approximating an adequate education. What's more, these centers were open no more than three days a week—and for half a day at that. The curriculum was "little more than a scant program of reading, singing and discussion," said the newspaper.

Once again, black parents—in one case with the determined "Fighting Preacher," Reverend L. Francis Griffin, as the plaintiff—hauled Virginia back to court. But as the *Washington Post* reported, when such lawsuits hit, Prince Edward County supervisors simply "denied that the Virginia constitution requires the operation of public schools in any county."

In the end, the US Supreme Court handed down two unequivocal decisions that forced the schools to reopen. Even then, we read in *Brown's Battleground*, local and state authorities "employed every weapon in their arsenal to ensure that the newly reopened system remained segregated, impoverished and academically substandard."

The most popular method of foot-dragging was the school board's freedom-of-choice plan. This ensured that white parents could move their children away from any school "threatened" with desegregation. The result was that by 1969, Prince Edward County schools were 98 percent black, and, once again, starved of resources. *Stall and defy* had transformed into *stall and undermine*, but the results were the same: devastating.

During the series of court cases swirling around Prince Edward County, a judge had noted that "an interrupted education of one year or even six months at that age places a serious handicap upon a child, which the average one may not overcome." The federal government agreed and in 1963 backed the privately funded Free School Association, which held classes in several of the county's closed schools, serving as an educational bridge to get the black children of Prince Edward County academically ready for when the public schools finally reopened.

But it was too late for many children.

Take John Hurt. He "did not attend school during the four years of the closings, which began when he was roughly nine years old," wrote Christopher Bonastia in his book *Southern Stalemate: Five Years without Public Education in Prince Edward County, Virginia.* When young Hurt finally went to a Free School, it was "just embarrassing" to sit in a classroom and look at an assignment, unable to do anything more than write his name at the top of the page. He had two crippling words to describe himself: "very dumb."

The psychological devastation was equally debilitating and long-lasting. Henry Cabarrus recalled one of Prince Edward County's white officials declaring that he would "rather his children be baked in the oven" than go to a desegregated school. Cabarrus, fourteen when the county's schools closed, was taken aback. "When you have such strong white resistance against you as a person," he told the *Washington Post* in 2006, "such that they can take away the most fundamental thing—education—if someone can take that away from you, your esteem is so small that . . . you're always looking over your shoulder for who is going to attack or criticize."

Prince Edward County is emblematic of the way that systematized racism not only destroys black lives but also undermines the very strength of the United States. As thousands of black children were left behind educationally, the economy was beginning a seismic transformation that would require even more from its citizens. Factory jobs were rapidly disappearing. By the time Prince Edward County finally implemented at least parts of *Brown* in the 1970s, the heyday of industrial America, where gainful employment had not required a strong education—just a strong back—was already well over. The knowledge-based economy was taking hold.

This new economy was primed for those who had had the

benefit of years of good schools and, in particular, for whites who had a well-funded public-school system that went all the way through the twelfth grade and graduated the lion's share of them as college-ready.

By contrast, countless black people who had suffered crummy schools and lapses in their education were now forced to face this cold, hard new economy with neither the necessary education nor technology-based work skills.

It was not just black America, however, that suffered the cost of this waste of human lives and talent. The brutally relentless tactics of *stall and defy*, then *stall and undermine*—tactics that went on for at least four decades—left the United States with millions of citizens who lacked the education needed to be competitive in a global, technology-driven economy. This, in turn, left the United States lagging far behind other developed countries and placed the nation at enormous economic risk.

White leaders in the South saw no such thing. They prided themselves as defenders of the Constitution and saviors of states' rights against a federal Leviathan. In their minds, they were patriots not racists. As Bonastia wrote of Prince Edward County officials: they maintained that "black parents were to blame for the interruption of their children's education, since blacks had chosen integration over education." Like others, these whites "painted the federal courts and the NAACP as the aggressors," we read in *Brown's Battleground*.

And in the battle, the NAACP was most definitely in the crosshairs.

With the launch of Sputnik I in 1957, Russia was seen as edging ahead in the Space Race. President Eisenhower dedicated new funding to education to ensure that the United States would make strides in technology, too, but school segregation limited students'—and the country's—ability to move forward.

12

THE NAACP AND SPUTNIK

BECAUSE THE NATIONAL ASSOCIATION FOR THE Advancement of Colored People was supposedly at the epicenter of the tumult and rebellion in the South, the next round in the chamber of Massive Resistance had the NAACP's name all over it. "There was nothing abstract about the South's hatred of the NAACP at that time," wrote Roy Wilkins in his autobiography, *Standing Fast*.

Starting in 1956, legislatures from Virginia to Texas passed laws that banned the association from operating within their states' borders.

Southern states also went after the NAACP with a pernicious use of the charge of barratry: the offense of instigating baseless lawsuits for the purpose of making money or mere harassment. The NAACP's formidable legal team was thus cast as nothing but fraudsters who cajoled unwitting and amoral people into going along with dubious lawsuits alleging violations of constitutional rights. Not only did the cynical enforcement of barratry statutes stop the association from providing legal counsel to those taking the brunt of Jim Crow, but it prevented the NAACP from giving financial support to those suing the state as well.

Southern governments also tried to crush the association by demanding that it either hand over or publicly post its membership lists. If the NAACP had complied, it would have put a bull's-eye on every one of its members. Whites could retaliate against a member of the NAACP in any number of ways. Shopkeepers or factory owners could fire people, for example. Men and women known to belong to NAACP could also be targeted for violence.

The association refused to surrender its membership lists. For that, it faced a series of injunctions and fines, some totaling one hundred thousand dollars.

If that were not enough, in 1956 Attorney General Eugene Cook of Georgia capriciously decided that the NAACP was, despite its tax-exempt status, a for-profit organization—and it owed the state a whopping $17,000 in back taxes, or the equivalent in 2016 of $150,000. Cook then insisted, and a local judge agreed, that until the NAACP paid what it supposedly owed Georgia, the association couldn't operate in the state. Just to drive home the point, authorities arrested J. H. Calhoun, the head of the NAACP's branch in Atlanta.

Similarly, in 1956, Texas's attorney general John Ben Shepperd had Texas Rangers and state highway patrolmen raid local NAACP offices in search of proof of a failure to pay taxes and engagement in any illegal political activity. Despite an utter lack of evidence, a local judge issued the requisite injunction to put the NAACP out of business in Texas. It was also in 1956 that the

NAACP was banned in Alabama (unable to resume operations until 1964). For eight years, at the peak of the Civil Rights Movement, which had been spurred on by *Brown*, the association was effectively crippled below the Mason-Dixon Line.

Meanwhile the recalcitrant South swaddled itself in the American flag, portraying its efforts as the last holdout of patriotism. White sons of the South combined two of their favorite villains—the NAACP and the Communist Party, USA—into one treasonous behemoth, which they unveiled during a series of congressional and state hearings.

After World War II the United States and the Soviet Union, along with their allies, entered a "Cold War"—a war of propaganda, ideology, and economic wrangling. Which superpower would be the victor? Whose ideology would lead the world? The capitalist United States or the communist Soviet Union? Many Americans looked upon communists, called "Reds," with fear and loathing. In the early 1950s Wisconsin senator Joseph McCarthy began conducting hearings designed to ferret out communists and communist sympathizers. McCarthy's model was the House Un-American Activities Committee (HUAC), created in the 1930s to investigate people who were supposedly subversive and un-American, was also active during the Red Scare of the late 1940s and the 1950s. People found to be or suspected of being communist were physically attacked, shunned, fired from jobs, and forced to flee their homes. Lives were ruined.

It was in this climate that Mississippi senator James O. Eastland claimed that *Brown* "was the result of communist manipulation," as Bartley put it in *The Rise of Massive Resistance*. Drawing on questionable records from the infamous House Un-American Activities Committee, the Mississippi senator insisted that the scholars the association had relied on in *Brown*, such as sociologist E. Franklin Frazier, had "no less than 18 citations" before HUAC.

Arkansas representative Ezekiel Gathings, wrote Bartley, "filled forty pages of the *Congressional Record* with charges against the NAACP, asserting that 89 of its 193 officeholders during 1954 had been cited by" HUAC.

Sensitivity to such arguments, no matter how false they were, only increased when a Cold War crisis hit in 1957.

On Friday, October 4, of that year, America's sense of nuclear invincibility was shattered by the faint *beep, beep, beep* sound heard over a radio receiver. The Soviets had successfully launched a satellite, something the United States had yet to achieve. The Soviet satellite, Sputnik, circled Earth every ninety-six minutes. Up until then, the threat of the Soviet Union's nuclear arsenal had been lessened by its seeming inability to send a payload of destruction across the Pacific or Atlantic Oceans. With Sputnik, traveling thousands of miles had been reduced to the equivalent of crossing the street.

The *New Republic* feared that Sputnik was "proof of the fact that the Soviet Union has gained a commanding lead in certain vital sectors of the race for world scientific and technological supremacy."

The *New York Times* glumly reported that the Department of Defense's missile experts were "shaken by Sputnik," because it was "evidence of Soviet superiority in rocketry."

The *Washington Post* intoned, "This is confirmation, if any really is needed, of Soviet progress with the intercontinental ballistic missile and intermediate range ballistic missile."

The grave consequences were not just military. The entire structure of US Cold War foreign policy was threatened. "Let no one mistake the political significance of the Soviet accomplishment," continued the *Post*'s gloomy editorial. "It will have a strong psychological effect in intimidating wavering allies and uncommitted countries, for it will seem to say that the Soviet Union is irresistible." Americans feared that their allies and potential allies might go over to the Soviet Union's side.

This was a national security crisis.

In April 1957, six months before Sputnik, President Eisenhower commissioned a blue-ribbon panel. H. Rowan Gaither, head of the Ford Foundation, was its chairman. The Gaither committee's task was to prepare for the National Security Council an analysis on the state of America's military preparedness. The top-secret *Gaither Report* hit the president's desk on November 7, 1957, a month after the Soviets sent up Sputnik—and three days after the Soviets launched Sputnik II, which had a much heavier payload (and a dog named Laika, who, sadly, died while on board).

As for the *Gaither Report*, it did not remain hush-hush for long.

There were leaks.

The reaction to the report was as thunderous as that to the Soviet satellite itself. It detailed America's shocking descent into "a second-class power," wrote Chalmers Roberts, a *Washington Post* reporter.

Newspaper editorials peppered President Eisenhower with criticism for his do-nothingness. "Two Sputniks cannot sway

Eisenhower," charged the *New York Post*. The consensus was that if things didn't change soon, the United States would not be able to recover.

What did Eisenhower do?

For one, in the summer of 1958 he signed an act that established the National Aeronautics and Space Administration (NASA). The Space Race was on. And in the rush to get on par with and then overtake the Soviet Union, there was a scramble to produce a better-educated America.

Many Americans agreed that the Cold War defeat represented by the success of Sputnik I and II could be traced right back to the schoolhouse door.

Some pointed to the trend toward progressive education and the lack of attention to the basics, especially math and science.

Most, however, identified the source of the problem as the unconscionable waste of intellectual talent as poor and unmotivated youth failed to go on to college.

Eisenhower now asserted that the United States had to do everything it could to prevent "the loss of a student with real ability." It was vital that this generation of American youth get the education necessary to be "equipped to live in the age of intercontinental ballistic missiles."

Along with the president, other politicians, as well as educators and pundits, hammered on this imperative against waste, arguing that the hundreds of thousands of young people who did not go to college were being "lost" to the nation.

Eisenhower was sure the answer was the National Defense Education Act, a plan to pour hundreds of millions of federal dollars into the nation's schools, colleges, and universities to bolster science and math education and create the citizenry necessary to fight the Cold War.

Alabama congressman Carl Elliott, who would take the lead in the crusade to transform education in the United States by backing the National Defense Education Act, argued that "in the context of critical national needs . . . a valuable national resource must not be lost through lack of action." And he warned: "Whatever happens in America's classrooms during the next fifty years will eventually happen to America."

What was happening to millions of students in America's classrooms in 1957, as Elliott well knew, was the direct outcome of Jim Crow. The long shadow it cast on a nation struggling to produce enough scientists and engineers should have signaled a turning point in the war on *Brown*: an acknowledgment that schools with no libraries and no labs had no chance of training the next generation of inventors and theoreticians. Grappling with America's trenchant refusal to open up the doors to quality education, *Time* magazine announced that the "gap between what the Negro now achieves and what he might achieve indicates that he is the nation's most wasted resource."

For all his hand-wringing, Representative Elliott was not about to do anything to repair the threat to national security posed by a system that deliberately starved millions of its citizens of adequate education. While he was clear that the nation had to "mobilize [its] brainpower, including schoolchildren and undergraduate and graduate students, on an emergency basis," Elliott nevertheless held that maintaining racial segregation (and the built-in inequality that came with it) was more critical to the nation.

So, while bills for the National Defense Education Act bounced through Congress, seeking ways to provide unprecedented federal financial support to schools and universities, Elliott, along with his fellow Alabamian senator Lister Hill, both signers of that Southern Manifesto, were insistent that any movement on education funding—even if for national security—could not dismantle Jim Crow or penalize Southern schools and universities for refusing to integrate.

The Alabamians had a strong ally in Eisenhower. Before *Brown* the president had voiced great skepticism about the validity of integration that did not spring organically from, say, Mississippi or South Carolina. He was a states' rights man. In his eyes, the US Supreme Court was wrong to insert the federal government into local race relations. After the *Brown* decision, in a 1957 letter to his friend Edward "Swede" Hazlett, Eisenhower said that "no other single event has so disturbed the domestic scene in many years as did the Supreme Court's decision of 1954 in the school segregation case."

To find some manner of peace, the president laid out his priorities: empathy for how hard it would be for the South to jettison its way of life on the basis of a "mere decision of the Supreme Court" and respect for the Supreme Court's authority.

The president hoped to reconcile the two. "The plan of the Supreme Court to accomplish integration gradually and sensibly," he told Hazlett, "seems to me to provide the only possible answer if we are to consider on the one hand the customs and fears of a great section of our population, and on the other the binding effect that Supreme Court decisions must have on all of us if our form of government is to survive and prosper." Noticeably absent from the president's list of priorities were the rights and educational needs of black people.

Thus, as the National Defense Education Act was being debated and crafted, Eisenhower had no intention of using tens of millions of federal dollars to finally gain compliance with *Brown* by "threatening to withhold funds from segregated educational institutions," explained Barbara Barksdale Clowse in her book *Brainpower for the Cold War: The Sputnik Crisis and National Defense Education Act of 1958.*

The White House's icy stance was affirmed by the attorney for the Department of Health, Education, and Welfare (HEW) Richard Conley. During House-Senate conference proceedings on the proposed National Defense Education Act, Conley explained that although *Brown* was the law of the land, his agency had no intention of enforcing that ruling. "He stated that integration would not be a precondition for obtaining funds unless the Congress decided it should be," we read in *Brainpower for the Cold War.*

How likely was that, given that Southerners dominated Congress?

Thus, the University of Georgia, the University of Mississippi, and the University of Alabama, among other universities in the South, could continue to deny young black men and women admission on the basis of race and still receive federal funding.

Assured that *Brown* would have no effect on the proposed National Defense Education Act, Elliott and Hill, desperate to pour federal dollars into white schools in Alabama, marshaled all their legislative wizardry to guide the bill through both houses of Congress.

And so, when House Resolution 13247 successfully emerged, allocating $183 million in 1959 and another $222 million in 1960 to schools and universities for fellowships, facility upgrades, and state-of-the-art equipment, the desperate conditions of millions of young black people faced remained in full force.

Given Congressman Elliott's prediction that whatever happened in America's classrooms in the 1950s would determine what the United States would look like half a century later, the deliberate omission of black people from the National Defense Education Act bore its bitter fruit. In 2004, fifty years after *Brown*, the *Journal of Blacks in Higher Education* reported that not one black person earned a PhD in astronomy or astrophysics, for example. In fact, of the 2,100 PhDs awarded in forty-three different fields in the natural sciences, not one went to a black person.

The refusal to implement *Brown* throughout the South even in the face of Sputnik I and II—not only as the law or as simple humanity might have dictated but also as demanded by national interest and patriotism—compromised and undermined American strength. Now, in the twenty-first century, the sector of the US economy that accounts for more than *50 percent* of our sustained economic expansion, science and engineering, is relying on an ever-dwindling skilled-and-educated workforce. According to Rodney C. Adkins, senior vice president of IBM, at one point, "about 40% of the world's scientists and engineers resided in the U.S." Sadly "that number [had] shrunk to about 15%" by 2012.

The 1950s should be seen as a fateful moment in America when history failed to turn and alter the trajectory of the nation.

Brown held out hope to millions desperately seeking a quality education.

Since the days of enslavement, black people have fought to gain access to quality education.

Education can be transformative.

Education reshapes the health outcomes of a people.

Education breaks the cycle of poverty.

Education improves housing conditions.

Education raises the standard of living.

Perhaps most meaningfully, educational attainment significantly increases voter participation. In short, education strengthens a democracy.

As if sensing this threat, white opposition careened from the Massive Resistance of disenfranchisement, interposition, school closures, and harassment of the NAACP to the passive resistance of pupil-placement laws, residential segregation, token integration, and "neighborhood schools." In Little Rock, when the schools were forced to reopen, the most liberal member of the school board, sounding eerily similar to Georgia's attorney general Cook, proposed using the law to undercut *Brown* and limit how integrated Little Rock schools would be. He argued that pupil-assignment plans, using the same factors that Mississippi had considered— "ability," "whether a good fit or not"—could ensure that most blacks stayed right where they were. Meanwhile, a handful of blacks could be enrolled in white schools; just enough to "satisfy the federal courts," as Sondra Gordy put it in *Finding the Lost Year*, but at the same time, "small enough to satisfy the reluctant and vocal whites in the community."

This tactical shift from *stall and defy* to *stall and undermine* effectively jammed up court dockets for more than forty years, as black people struggled to nail down a moving target whose goal had not changed: stop black advancement.

In the war on *Brown*, black people were not the only ones who took a hit. The states that fought *Brown* tooth and nail all fall today in the bottom quartile of state rankings for educational attainment, per capita income, and quality of health.

Prince Edward County, in particular, bears the scars of a place that saw fit to fight the Civil War right into the middle of the twentieth century. Certainly it is no accident that, in 2013, despite a knowledge-based, technology-driven global economy, the number one occupation in the county seat of Farmville was "cook and food preparation worker." Nor is it any accident that in 2013, while 9.9 percent of white households in the county made less than ten thousand dollars in annual income, fully *32.9 percent* of black households fell below that threshold. The insistence on destroying *Brown*, and thus the viability of the nation's schools and the quality of education children receive regardless of where they live, was and truly is an American tragedy.

Many civil rights icons were in attendance as President Lyndon B. Johnson signed the Civil Rights Act, including Martin Luther King Jr, pictured above shaking Johnson's hand. Those opposed to the act complained once again that civil rights progression wasn't correcting injustices but instead was granting blacks special preferential treatment.

13

ROLLING BACK CIVIL RIGHTS

THE CIVIL RIGHTS MOVEMENT WAS SO MUCH more than Rosa Parks refusing to give up her bus seat in Montgomery, Alabama, on December 1, 1955, or Martin Luther King Jr.'s "I Have a Dream" speech on the National Mall before two hundred and fifty thousand people on August 28, 1963.

The movement was a series of hard-fought, locally organized campaigns, supported at times by national organizations such as King's Southern Christian Leadership Conference (SCLC), shining the spotlight on gross inequalities in employment, accommodations, and the right to vote.

Adopting the strategy of nonviolence, black people skillfully used the media to expose the horrors of Jim Crow to the world— from snarling dogs lunging at children in Birmingham to schoolteachers yanked onto the concrete for trying to register to vote in Selma to four little girls in a Birmingham church dynamited right after a Sunday school lesson on "A Love That Forgives."

This Civil Rights Movement was a battle, as the SCLC noted, "to redeem the soul of America."

In 1957 Eisenhower signed the first civil rights legislation since Reconstruction: the Civil Rights Act of 1957. Among other things, it established a civil rights division in the US Justice Department and empowered its chief, the US attorney general, to take action to protect black people's voting rights. Three years later came the Civil Rights Act of 1960, which also sought to protect the vote. It established penalties for anyone interfering with another person's attempt to vote or register to vote.

These acts were so ineffectual that mass disenfranchisement and overt discrimination remained virtually untouched. So black Americans and their white allies continued to put their bodies on the line.

Finally, in the summer of 1964, Congress passed a comprehensive, game-changing civil rights bill. It sought to stamp out discrimination based on race, color, national origin, religion, and sex on many fronts, from education and employment to voting and places of public accommodation such as parks and restaurants. Martin Luther King Jr., the NAACP's Roy Wilkins, and Dorothy Height, president of the National Council of Negro Women were among the great crowd of witnesses in the White House when President Lyndon Johnson signed this landmark bill into law on July 2, 1964.

A year later, on August 6, 1965, President Johnson signed the Voting Rights Act (VRA) of 1965.

Literacy tests—forbidden!

Federal examiners could take charge of voter registration in places where voter suppression was most horrendous!

And there was the VRA's Section 5: where voter suppression was rampant, no new voting rules and regulations could be introduced without the approval of the District Court for the District of Columbia or the US attorney general.

"This law covers many pages," said President Johnson shortly before he signed the bill into law. "But the heart of the act is plain. Wherever, by clear and objective standards, States and counties are using regulations, or laws, or tests to deny the right to vote, then they will be struck down."

The impact of this civil rights struggle had been slow but significant. Inequality had begun to lessen. Incomes had started to rise. Job and educational opportunities had expanded. Given the power of this iconic movement, the descent into what Michelle Alexander dubbed the "the New Jim Crow" should have been virtually impossible. But just as with Reconstruction, the Great Migration, and the *Brown* decision, black advances set the gears of white opposition in motion. The desire to crush the promise embedded in the Civil Rights Act of 1964 and the Voting Rights Act of 1965 was intense. Yet again, the United States moved from the threshold of democracy to the betrayal of it.

But before the rollback on civil rights got underway, what the Civil Rights Movement was really "about" had to be redefined.

White people opposed to liberty and justice for all reduced centuries of oppression and brutality to the harmless symbolism of a bus seat and a water fountain. So when Whites Only signs came down, inequality had supposedly disappeared. Also magically removed by this interpretation were up to $24 trillion in multi-generational devastation that blacks had suffered in lost wages,

IN BRIEF:
THE CIVIL RIGHTS ACT OF 1964

TITLE I: Voting Rights
Prohibited selective use of voter registration requirements.
(If black would-be voters are required to take a literacy test,
for example, white would-be voters must take the same
test.)

**TITLE II: Discrimination in Places of Public
Accommodation**
Prohibited discrimination (including segregation) in places
open to the general public, such as hotels, restaurants, the-
aters, and stadiums, based on race, color, religion, or national
origin.

TITLE III: Desegregation of Public Facilities
Empowered the US attorney general, the nation's chief law
officer, to bring a lawsuit on behalf of people discriminated
against by a facility run by a state or a municipality (such as a
state park).

TITLE IV: Desegregation of Public Schools
Empowered the US attorney general to sue a school board
or a public college in cases of discrimination based on race,
color, religion, or national origin.

TITLE V: Commission on Civil Rights
Expanded the role of the Commission on Civil Rights (created in 1957, chiefly to investigate violations of voting
rights) to include looking into legal developments related
to discrimination in other areas of life, such as housing and
employment.

TITLE VI: Discrimination in Programs that Receive Federal Funds

Banned discrimination on account of race, color, or national origin in any entity (from a government agency to a university) receiving federal funds.

TITLE VII: On Equal Employment Opportunity

Prohibited workplace discrimination (from refusal to hire to wages) on account of a person's race, color, religion, sex, or national origin. It also established the US Equal Employment Opportunity Commission (EEOC) to enforce the law.

TITLE VIII: Registration and Voting Statistics

Authorized the Secretary of Commerce to compile data on voting in whatever localities the Commission on Civil Rights dictated.

TITLE IX: Removal of Civil Rights Cases from State to Federal Courts

Authorized the US attorney general to remove a civil rights case from state court (where the presiding judge may be prosegregation) to a federal court.

TITLE X: Community Relations Service

Established a Community Relations Service to help communities (and the people in them) resolve issues arising from discrimination based on race, color, or national origin.

TITLE XI: Miscellaneous

Set the penalty for anyone found guilty of trying to obstruct or interfere with what the Civil Rights Act is intended to accomplish: a fine of no more than $1,000 or imprisonment for no more than six months.

stolen land, educational impoverishment, and housing inequalities. It was as if all of that never happened. As Patrick Buchanan, conservative pundit and adviser to several presidents, would assert in 2008: "America has been the best country on earth for black folks. It was here that 600,000 black people, brought from Africa in slave ships, grew into a community of 40 million, were introduced to Christian salvation, and reached the greatest levels of freedom and prosperity blacks have ever known."

Similarly, chattel slavery, which built the United States' inordinate wealth, molted into an institution in which few if any whites had ever benefited because their families were never

KEY PARTS OF THE VOTING RIGHTS ACT OF 1965

SECTION 2 is an overall prohibition against hurdles and obstacles designed to keep people from voting because of their race or color.

SECTION 3 allowed for the appointment of federal examiners to oversee voter registration in places where voting rights need to be enforced.

SECTION 4 created a formula for identifying places that had a terrible record of racial discrimination when it came to voting—localities that would be subject to federal scrutiny as mapped out in Section 5 of the act.

The covered jurisdictions would be subject to section 5 of the Voting Rights Act of 1965. Section 4 also established that places could be released from federal scrutiny if, after at least five years, they proved that they had not engaged in anything untoward when it came to voting and voting registration.

slaveholders. This was a denial of white privilege enjoyed whether or not a white person's ancestors were slaveholders, whether or not a white person's ancestors were even born in the United States, whether or not a white person was rich or poor.

Once the need for the Civil Rights Movement was minimized and history rewritten, initiatives like President Johnson's Great Society and Affirmative Action, which were developed to make amends—atone—for hundreds of years of violent and corrosive repression, were easily characterized as reverse discrimination against hardworking whites and a "government handout that lazy black people 'choose' to take rather than work," as

SECTION 5 Jurisdictions covered in Section 4 could make no changes to voting procedures without "preclearance," that is, an okay from the Department of Justice or the US District Court for the District of Columbia.

The remaining fourteen sections of the Voting Rights Act of 1965 dealt with, among other things, the role of federal examiners and poll watchers, the abolition of the poll tax, and the penalty for violating certain provisions of the act (up to $5000, up to five years imprisonment, or both).

Black Americans were not the only beneficiaries of the Voting Rights Act of 1965. One provision was aimed at removing obstacles to the vote from the path of Puerto Ricans educated in specified schools where English was not the primary language of instruction. It is because of later amendments to the Voting Rights Act that certain places have notices, ballots, and other election-related material in Spanish, Russian, Korean, and other languages.

Stephanie Greco Larson put it in *Media and Minorities: The Politics of Race in News and Entertainment.*

"Will you join in the battle to build the Great Society," President Lyndon Johnson had asked on May 22, 1964, of his audience—of America—"to prove that our material progress is only the foundation on which we will build a richer life of mind and spirit?" Johnson uttered this challenge in a commencement address at the University of Michigan.

President Johnson's Great Society programs included Head Start, an early-childhood-development program for low-income families that tackled not only education but also health and nutrition. The Great Society produced initiatives to get more young folks working, such as Job Corps Youth Training Program and Volunteers in Service to America (VISTA)—later absorbed into AmeriCorps in 1993, through which young people eager to be change agents fanned out to enrichment programs in impoverished communities. With the Great Society the food stamp program went from a pilot program to a permanent one. Out of compassion for the low-income elderly and other poor people came free or low-cost health insurance through Medicare and Medicaid.

Of course, and often ignored by critics of the Great Society, plenty of white people benefited from these offerings.

As for Affirmative Action, initially launched by President Kennedy's 1961 Executive Order 10925 to stamp out discrimination—based on race, color, religion, sex, or national origin—white women have benefited the most. The critics of Affirmative Action never said a mumbling word about all the years of preferential treatment for white people in higher education such as legacy admissions, where children of alums get a leg up.

The second key maneuver in rolling back civil rights was to redefine racism itself.

Confronted with headlines about KKK rallies and jackbooted sheriffs, white authority transformed those damning images of white supremacy into the *sole* definition of racism. This simple but wickedly brilliant shift served multiple purposes.

First and foremost, it was conscience soothing. The whittling down of racism to sheet-wearing goons enveloped white people who were not members of the Klan or groups like it in a cloud of racial innocence. Such people, although hostile to black advancement, could see and project themselves as the "kind of upstanding white citizen[s]" who were "positively outraged at the tactics of the Ku Klux Klan," wrote Alexander in *The New Jim Crow*.

The focus on the Klan also helped to tag racism as an *individual* aberration rather than something *systemic, institutional*, and *pervasive*. What's more, isolating racism to only its most virulent and visible form allowed politicians and judges to push for policies that *seemed* to meet the standard of America's new civil rights norms while at the same time working to undermine and destabilize these norms, all too often leaving black communities ravaged.

The objective was to contain and neutralize the victories of the Civil Rights Movement by painting a picture of a "colorblind," equal opportunity society whose doors were now wide open. All black people had to do was take the initiative and walk on through.

The recasting of the Civil Rights Movement, of slavery, of

racism left many whites fuming. Second- and third-generation Polish Americans, Italian Americans, and other white ethnics seethed that, whereas their own immigrant parents and grandparents had had to work their way out of ghettos, blacks were getting a government-sponsored free ride to the good life on the backs of honest, hardworking white Americans.

Some Northern whites began to complain that civil rights apparently only applied to black people. One unnamed US senator confided, "I'm getting mail from white people saying 'Wait a minute, we've got some rights too.'"

By the 1968 presidential election, white opposition had once more coalesced into an effective force.

Huey Newton, right, and Bobby Seale, left, founded the Black Panther Party. While the Civil Rights Movement had focused primarily on the injustices blacks faced in the South, the Black Panthers aimed to address the daily discriminations and brutalities blacks across the entire nation faced. Their policies of self-defense in the face of violence and their open embrace of black power intensified white backlash following the Civil Rights Act.

14

"LIKE YOUR WHOLE WORLD DEPENDED ON IT"

DURING HIS 1968 PRESIDENTIAL BID, ALABAMA governor George Wallace very much understood white resentment above the Mason-Dixon Line. He had experienced a startling epiphany in 1963, after trying to keep two young black people, Vivian Malone and James Hood, from enrolling in Alabama state's flagship university at Tuscaloosa. For that act of defiance, Governor Wallace received more than one hundred thousand congratulatory telegrams, *half* of which came from above the Mason-Dixon Line. Right then he had a revelation. Journalist Douglas Kiker imagined Wallace exclaiming, "They all hate black people, all of them. They're all afraid, all of them. Great God! That's it! They're all Southern! The whole United States is Southern!"

"Segregation now . . . segregation tomorrow . . . segregation forever," Wallace had declared in his 1963 Inaugural Address after he won Alabama's gubernatorial race.

In 1968 that kind of talk would not do.

So in his bid for the presidency, Wallace mastered the use of race-neutral language to explain what was at stake for disgruntled working-class whites, particularly those whose neighborhoods butted right up against black enclaves. To the thousands, sometimes tens of thousands, who came to his campaign rallies in Detroit, Boston, San Francisco, New York, Chicago, and San Diego, Wallace played on the ever-present fear that black people were breaking out of crime-filled ghettos and moving "into 'our' streets, 'our' schools, 'our' neighborhoods," as Dan T. Carter summed it up in his book *From George Wallace to Newt Gingrich*.

For working-class whites whose hold on some semblance of the American dream was becoming increasingly tenuous as the economy buckled under pressure from financing both the Great Society and the Vietnam War, this was naturally upsetting. Black gains, it was assumed, could come only at white peoples' expense. Not surprisingly, polls showed that as black people achieved greater access to their citizenship rights, white unease mounted. In their 1967 book, *Black and White*, a study on racial attitudes in America, pollsters Louis Harris and William Brink reported that by 1966, 85 percent of whites were certain that "the pace of civil-rights progress was too fast. Only a year before, the number who had felt Negroes were moving too fast had been 49 percent. A year before that, only 34 percent of all white people felt that way."

In 1966, too fast.

By the mid-1960s black Americans' median family income was only 55 percent of that of whites. The black unemployment rate was nearly twice as high as the white unemployment rate. What's more, by 1965, just 27 percent of black adults had completed four years of high school. More than 50 percent of whites twenty-five years and over had done so.

Too fast?

Black Americans simply refused to accept those disparities as natural. They insisted that inequality was the result of a series of public policies that must be changed. Therefore, they continued to file lawsuits for equality of opportunity in education, employment, and in other areas of life. (Passage of, say, the Civil Rights Act of 1964 was one thing. Making companies, for example, abide by it was another thing.) In pursuit of justice and fair play black people also elected black men and women to city councils, mayorships, and other public offices in large numbers.

Black resolve to dismantle racial inequality led one white woman in Dayton, Ohio, to assert, "Oh, they are so forward. If you give them your finger, they'll take your hand."

White angst and rage rose further with the more overtly militant shift in the black freedom movement's pursuit of justice and equality of opportunity.

After more than a decade of beatings, jailings, and killings, the ethos of nonviolent protest had begun to wear thin, especially among the youth involved in the demonstrations. Remember, too, that the Civil Rights Movement initially zeroed in on the plight of black people in the South. For the most part, it did not address the discrimination that millions of black people faced in the urban North, Midwest, and West. Thus, nonviolence gave way to an ethos of self-defense, best articulated by the Black Panther Party, a group founded in Oakland, California, in 1966.

The Panthers openly brandished guns and challenged the

police. The goal of desegregration, so fundamental to the SCLC and the NAACP, was now forced to openly compete with the more sharply articulated demands of black nationalism and black power.

Soon, in response to police brutality, rioting consumed parts of Newark, Detroit, Los Angeles, and Cleveland. This intensified the white backlash. It also allowed white people who were already exasperated by what they perceived as threats to the status quo to claim their feelings were justified.

During his bid for the presidency in 1968, Richard Nixon, a former vice president (under Eisenhower) and California senator, tapped into this general white resentment just like George Wallace had a few years before. To make the most of it, Nixon's handlers came up with the "Southern Strategy." This plan was aimed at pulling into the Grand Old Party, or GOP, as the Republican Party is nicknamed, not only white Democratic voters from below the Mason-Dixon Line but also those aggrieved whites who lived in northern working-class neighborhoods.

Using strategic dog-whistle appeals (that is, coded messages) about crime and welfare for example, to trigger knee-jerk anti-black responses, Nixon succeeded in defining and maligning the Democrats as the party of black people, without once having to actually say the words.

Nixon, therefore, framed America's issues as "excesses" caused by, among other things, "bleeding heart liberalism." The recent Civil Rights Act and the Voting Rights Act, he asserted, had removed the legal barriers to equality. They had also, he continued, raised unrealistic expectations in the black community. When equality didn't immediately emerge, he explained, lawlessness and rioting followed. On the presidential campaign trail, Nixon's basic mantra was that "it was both wrong and dangerous to make promises that cannot be fulfilled, or to raise hopes that come to nothing." The point, therefore, was to puncture black people's expectations.

That downward thrust would come through the iron fist of law and order. Crime and blackness soon became synonymous in a carefully constructed way. One of Nixon's campaign ads carefully avoided using pictures of black people as it showed cities burning, grainy images of protesters out in the streets, blood flowing, chaos shaking the very foundation of society, and then . . .

Silence.

As the screen faded to black, emblazoned with white lettering: THIS TIME VOTE LIKE YOUR WHOLE WORLD DEPENDED ON IT: NIXON.

After he screened the ad, Nixon enthusiastically told his staff that the commercial "hits it right on the nose. It's all about law and order and the damn Negro–Puerto Rican groups out there." Yet in the ad he didn't have to say so explicitly. It was crystal clear who was the threat. It was also crystal clear whose world depended on Richard Nixon for salvation.

Following his inauguration, President Nixon targeted what Kenneth O'Reilly called in his book *Nixon's Piano: Presidents and Racial Politics from Washington to Clinton* "two of the civil rights movement's greatest victories."

Activist Jimmie Lee Jackson was killed by police in 1965 during a peaceful voting rights protest. His death was an impetus for the march from Selma to Montgomery, Alabama, and the eventual passage of the Voting Rights Act. Here his casket is carried into Brown Chapel in Selma.

15

IN THE CROSSHAIRS: THE VRA

THE REPUBLICAN PARTY'S NEW SOUTHERN WING loathed the Voting Rights Act, empowering black Americans as it did through the ballot box.

President Richard Nixon's strategy—one that would play out well into the twenty-first century—was to "weaken the enforcement of civil rights laws," wrote Ari Berman in his book *Give Us the Ballot.*

And the VRA *was* vulnerable. It only passed because it contained the unprecedented provision that one component—Section Five—be renewed within five years. When President Nixon was sworn in as the nation's thirty-seventh president on January 20, 1969, the clock was definitely ticking.

A few months later, as the May–June 1969 VRA renewal hearings began, the Republican co-chair of the House Judiciary Committee, William McCulloch of Ohio, a civil rights advocate, explained that he had hoped the basic foundation of democracy—the vote—would now be accepted and honored. But "resistance to the program has been more subtle and more effective than I thought possible," said McCulloch. "A whole arsenal of racist weapons has been perfected."

In the wake of the VRA's passage, instead of outright denial of access to the ballot, the South had begun to dilute black electoral strength by rigging precinct boundaries: gerrymandering, remapping a district in such a way that gives one party a numeric advantage.

Southern states had also sought to weaken the black vote by changing the rules of the game when it came to certain offices. Mississippi, for example, had passed a series of laws that turned the elected position of school superintendent into a political appointee. With that, how likely would it be that a white school board hostile to black people would appoint someone committed to equality for *all* students to be school superintendent?

Virginia, which prior to the VRA had assigned election officials to help the illiterate vote, mandated that ballots had to be handwritten.

Did these changes violate Section 5 of the VRA, which requires that the US Department of Justice or the district court in DC to preapprove changes to election requirements in certain jurisdictions? The Southern states that employed these tactics argued no. They maintained that Section 5 only applied to mechanisms that directly affected access to the ballot box, such as the poll tax.

In *Allen v. State Board of Elections*, US Supreme Court chief justice Earl Warren stopped Mississippi and Virginia in their tracks.

The VRA was "aimed at the subtle, as well as the obvious, state regulations which have the effect of denying citizens their right to vote because of their race," Warren stated in delivering the majority opinion in this 7–2 decision of March 3, 1969.

Thus during the spring 1969 VRA renewal hearings, Representative McCulloch, therefore, noted in his support for renewal that it was painfully obvious that, "350 years of oppression cannot be eradicated in 5 years."

While McCulloch saw the need to protect the ballot box, Attorney General John Mitchell, who had served as director of Nixon's 1968 presidential run, announced that the Department of Justice, which he viewed as "an institution for law enforcement, not social improvement," opposed the VRA's renewal.

Why?

Mitchell claimed that it targeted, and therefore discriminated against, the South.

This upside-down framing of the VRA (and the sense that it was somehow not about the law but social engineering) purposely whitewashed the brutal electoral history of Jim Crow. It transformed ruthless perpetrators into innocent victims.

In addition to engaging in electoral shenanigans, more than a few Southern states had sanctioned or even fomented widespread terrorism against voting rights activists.

On September 25, 1961, Herbert Lee, who was helping to register black people in Amite County, was ambushed and executed by a Mississippi legislator, E. H. Hurt. A few years later, another black man, World War II veteran Louis Allen, a witness to Lee's murder, was treated to a shotgun blast that blew off his face. Both executions sent a signal that the death sentence awaited blacks who had the audacity to vote and help others do likewise.

And there were the bullet-riddled corpses of James Chaney (black), Andrew Goodman (white), and Michael Schwerner (white), bodies unearthed on August 4, 1964, after weeks spent beneath tons of dirt in Neshoba County, Mississippi. Their murders had served as a warning that those advocating the right to vote were, as one local woman scoffed, "just looking for trouble."

At a time when less than 1 percent of black people in Selma, Alabama, were registered to vote, there was the televised fury police officers unleashed on peaceful protesters—tear-gassed, whipped, trampled by horse-bound troopers—as these people tried to symbolically carry to the state capital of Montgomery the casket of slain black voting rights activist Jimmie Lee Jackson. Jackson had been killed by law enforcement on February 26, 1965.

The horror of that attempt to cross the Edmund Pettus bridge on that Sunday, March 7, 1965—Bloody Sunday—was punctuated two days later by the bludgeoning of white Unitarian minister Reverend James Reeb. He had come to Selma from Boston in support of voting rights. The reverend died of his wounds on March 11.

These are just a *few* of the atrocities, the crimes against humanity, that had compelled sane people to say, *Yes! A muscular Voting Rights Act is imperative.*

But for only five years?

Despite Attorney General Mitchell's insinuation, the VRA was neither capricious nor punitive. It was, as the Department of Justice noted, "targeted at those areas of the country where

Congress believed the potential for discrimination to be the greatest."

In 1966, in *South Carolina v. Katzenbach*, the US Supreme Court, in an 8–1 decision, affirmed the need for federal oversight, ruling that: "Congress had found that case-by-case litigation [based on the 1957 Civil Rights Act] was inadequate to combat wide-spread and persistent discrimination in voting, because of the inordinate amount of time and energy required to overcome the obstructionist tactics invariably encountered in these lawsuits. After enduring nearly a century of systematic resistance to the Fifteenth Amendment, Congress might well decide to shift the advantage of time and inertia from the perpetrators of the evil to its victims."

Indeed, the impact of the VRA was profound. For example, just prior to its passage, only 6.7 percent of Mississippi's black adults were registered to vote. Three years later that number had skyrocketed to 59.4 percent.

And where was President Nixon in the war on the VRA?

Because the VRA was clearly working, the first civil rights legislation Nixon sent to Congress proposed eliminating Section 5 and stretching the VRA's scope to the entire country.

Far from trying to disenfranchise black voters, Nixon disingenuously explained, the amended legislation sought simply to address an imbalance that, when other areas of the nation also discriminated against segments of their citizenry, left the South unfairly singled out.

What eventually became clear during the congressional hearings, however, was that Nixon's new "civil rights legislation" would create a wholly uncivil America. "With the entire nation covered," Attorney General Mitchell admitted, "it would be impossible for the Civil Rights Division of the Department of Justice to screen every voting change in every county in the nation." His staff would be unable to enforce the VRA at all. Those who believed their rights had been violated at the ballot box, Mitchell continued, just needed to go through the courts. In essence, Nixon's plan was to hurl black Americans and the nation back to the slow, litigious route carved out in the long-since-discredited Civil Rights Act of 1957.

During the VRA's renewal hearings of 1969, South Carolina senator Strom Thurmond embraced the Nixon administration's idea as he floated a narrative of racial innocence that minimized the terror and walled off the brutal history of disenfranchisement. Thurmond insisted that it was just wrong "to continually charge a state and a people with any alleged injustice that occurred many years ago."

The NAACP's Clarence Mitchell looked Thurmond in the eye and countered that the injustices were hardly "alleged" but, in fact, well documented.

"We could fill this room with the record of discrimination in the state of South Carolina," Mitchell informed the senator.

Nor was Thurmond's "many years ago" accurate. At every turn in the civil rights struggle, Mitchell asserted, "South Carolina has fought us all the way."

Indeed, in 1966, one year after the VRA passed, South Carolina went before the US Supreme Court, arguing that the act infringed on states' rights, had illegally inserted federal registrars in counties that had literacy tests (which had been outlawed by the VRA), and presumed the state's guilt simply because far into the twentieth century, only 0.8 percent of South Carolina's voting-age black population was registered to vote.

As Mitchell well knew, the court's 1966 *South Carolina v. Katzenbach* decision dismantled every one of the state's arguments and found the VRA constitutional. "But now that it appears we have won," Mitchell observed in his exchange with Thurmond, "we don't want to have a situation develop where the White House gives back to South Carolina all the rights to discriminate that we have succeeded in wresting from them."

The House and Senate agreed. Congress renewed the Voting Rights Act for another five years.

Thurgood Marshall was a staunch advocate for black children's right to education throughout his time on the US Supreme Court. He voiced a strong dissent in *San Antonio Independent School District v. Rodriguez,* where the Supreme Court failed to recognize the inherent racism in Texas's school-funding mechanisms.

BEATING DOWN *BROWN* (AGAIN!)

THE NIXON ADMINISTRATION TURNED ITS SIGHTS as well on *Brown*, which Massive Resistance and the subsequent tactic of *stall and undermine* had already weakened.

Almost fifteen years after the landmark Supreme Court decision, Mississippi had yet to desegregate its public-school system. When, on July 3, 1969, the federal court ordered the state to implement *Brown* by that fall, Nixon's attorney general, John Mitchell, and Nixon's secretary of Health, Education, and Welfare (HEW), Robert Finch, convinced the judges to reverse the decision because "time was too short and the administrative problems too difficult to accomplish . . . before the beginning of the 1969–1970 school year." Mississippi had already had more than a decade to develop a plan.

Nixon's four new appointments to the US Supreme Court would follow up on what Mitchell and HEW had done by eviscerating the constitutional right of black children to an education and then some.

As US Supreme Court vacancies opened on the bench, President Richard Nixon was drawn to the "law and order" writings of Warren Burger (appointed in 1969), who would replace Earl Warren as chief justice.

Nixon also approved of the "strict constructionists" decisions and Southern roots of Virginian Lewis Powell (appointed in 1971).

The president remained impressed by the "moderately conservative philosophy" and relative youth (at forty-seven years old) of William Rehnquist (appointed in 1971).

The most contentious battles had come over two of Nixon's Southern nominees. One was Clement Haynsworth, a "laundered segregationist," in the opinion of Joseph Rauh Jr., counsel at the time to the Leadership Conference on Civil Rights. The other was G. Harrold Carswell, who back in 1948 in Gordon, Georgia, before a chapter of the American Legion, had declared that "segregation of the races is proper and the only practical and correct way of life in our states."

After a bruising series of confirmation hearings, the Senate rejected both. Nixon then turned to his default choice, a Northerner, Harry Blackmun (appointed in 1970). The president reflected on his handiwork years later: "I consider my four appointments to the Supreme Court to have been among the most constructive and far-reaching actions of my presidency . . . The men I appointed shared my conservative judicial philosophy."

This was an understatement, even for Richard Nixon. The

court's subsequent decisions shut down access to quality education while allowing blatant racial discrimination to run rampant
in criminal procedures.

Two important 5–4 Supreme Court decisions in which Nixon's
appointees were in the slim but decisive majority undercut the
possibility that *Brown* would ever fully be implemented.

The first was the 1973 *San Antonio Independent School District v.
Rodriguez* case. Here parents from Edgewood, an impoverished
neighborhood that was 96 percent Mexican American and black,
took Texas to court because the school funding mechanism,
which relied on property taxes, generated such vastly different
amounts of money that equal educational opportunity was
impossible. Of course, the value of property, on which school funding was heavily based, derived from government enforcement of
residential segregation and discriminatory housing laws. There
were also a series of public-policy and zoning decisions such as
where to put landfills, erect sewage treatment plants, allow liquor
stores, and approve industrial plants—things that bring down
property values.

Zoning had had a particularly damaging effect on Edgewood. It had the lowest property value in the city. It also had the
lowest median income. So committed were the parents to their
children's education, however, that they voted for school levies
that taxed their property at the highest rate in the area. Even
then that generated only $21 per student per academic year.

In contrast, the affluent, predominately white San Antonio
neighborhood of Alamo Heights, with a property tax rate that
was significantly lower than Edgewood's, still produced enough

revenue to expend $307 per pupil. To put it another way: Alamo Heights secured nearly 1,500 percent more in funding with a significantly lower tax rate.

Seeing the inequity, the parents in Edgewood cried foul and sued.

The US District Court, using *Brown* as the template, agreed that something was wrong. In a survey of 110 school districts throughout the state, the judges found that while the wealthiest districts in Texas taxed their property at 31 cents per $100, the poorest were "burdened" with a rate of 70 cents. Still, the district court continued, even with their low tax rate, the rich districts netted $525 more per pupil than the poor districts did. Clearly, the judges concluded, Texas's funding scheme "makes education a function of the local property tax base."

The district court ruled that, "education is a fundamental right," that the state's use of "wealth" was a synonym for race and thus subject to judicial "strict scrutiny," and that Texas's funding scheme was irrational and violated the equal protection clause of the Fourteenth Amendment.

As the case moved up to the US Supreme Court, Texas pleaded racial innocence and claimed not only that it was meeting the bare minimum requirements for access to education but also that it could not and should not be held responsible for the differences between what poor districts and wealthy ones amassed.

Nixon's four appointees to the US Supreme Count—Warren E. Burger, Harry Blackmun, Lewis F. Powell, and William Rehnquist—as well as Potter Stewart (appointed by Eisenhower) agreed. In a March 1973 ruling that pulled the rug out from under *Brown*, they found that "there is no fundamental right to education in the Constitution." The justices concluded, too, that the state's funding scheme "did not systematically discriminate against all poor people in Texas." What's more, they maintained that because reliance on property taxes to fund schools was used across the country, the method was not "so irrational as to be invidiously discriminatory."

For the court, then, the funding scheme, in which, for example, Chicago allocated $5,265 for black pupils while the adjacent suburban school district of Niles appropriated $9,371 per student, was perfectly constitutional.

Despite the same kinds of rampant funding disparities that had led to *Brown*, Justice Lewis Powell declared that he saw no discriminatory public policy at all. With residential segregation no longer enforced by the government, whites and racial and ethnic minorities alike, he felt, were free to move wherever they wanted in search of better schools. The fact that most minorities— after centuries of government-enforced racism in education and employment—simply did not have the economic wherewithal to move was overlooked.

And so, even in the waning days of the Civil Rights Movement, entrenched, constitutionally unequal education was once again an important part of the nation's way of life.

"The Equal Protection Clause does not require absolute equality," Justice Powell declared in a powerfully worded edict, "or precisely equal advantages." What was at work here was *class*, not *race*; and class, unlike race, was not a "suspect category" that required "strict scrutiny," that is, the most stringent judicial review. If Texas had a rational basis for its property tax system, the justices concluded, then the mechanism met judicial standards, despite producing a 975 percent disparity in school funding between white and minority children in the state.

Fully recognizing the implications of *Rodriguez*, Associate Justice Thurgood Marshall, appointed to the High Court by President Johnson in August 1967, was apoplectic.

At the time, more than 40 percent of black children age fourteen and under in the nation lived with families below the poverty line, as compared with about 10 percent of white children. Under those circumstances, Marshall feared, black children wouldn't stand a chance. The *San Antonio Independent School District v. Rodriguez* decision, he wrote in his dissent, could "only be seen as a retreat" from a "commitment to equality of educational opportunity" as well as an "unsupportable" surrender to "a system which deprives children . . . of the chance to reach their full potential as citizens."

Marshall was simply dumbfounded that the majority of the justices acknowledged the existence of grossly different funding for schools across Texas but then, instead of focusing on the cause of that disparity, clumsily pirouetted around all of the state's supposed efforts to close the gaps. "The issue," Marshall explained, "is not whether Texas is doing its best to [improve] the worst features of a discriminatory scheme but, rather, whether the scheme itself is in fact unconstitutionally discriminatory."

Moreover, Justice Marshall found it the height of "absurdity" that Texas could actually argue there was no correlation between funding and school quality and then, from that faulty premise, deduce that there were "no discriminatory consequences for the children of the disadvantaged districts." Given the slew of amicus curiae briefs, that is written legal arguments from parties with a strong interest in a matter, that flooded the court in support of the way schools in Texas were funded, Marshall wryly observed that if "financing variations are so insignificant to educational quality it is difficult to understand why a number of our country's wealthiest school districts . . . have nevertheless zealously pursued its cause before this Court."

Marshall was equally unimpressed with Texas's tendency to parade before the justices stories of children who had excelled despite living in under-resourced districts as some sort of proof that funding was irrelevant. That a child could excel even when "forced to attend an underfunded school with poorer physical facilities, less experienced teachers, larger classes," and a number of other deficits compared with "a school with substantially more funds," Marshall barked, "is to the credit of the child not the State."

Rodriguez placed the burden solely on the backs of the most vulnerable, while walling off access to the necessary resources for quality education. It played beautifully into the "colorblind," post-civil-rights language of substituting economics for race, yet achieving a similar result: inequality.

The next year, Nixon's Supreme Court appointees landed yet another powerful blow to *Brown*. This time the case emerged out of the North, in Detroit, which, by the early 1970s, was a predominately black city surrounded by overwhelmingly white suburbs.

Detroit's K–12 system mirrored the racial geography, with virtually all the schools in the city more than 90 percent black. These schools were overcrowded, sometimes with classrooms holding as many as *fifty* students. Buildings were so decayed and unsafe that classes were taught in trailers parked on the school grounds. Vera Bradley, a black mother of two sons, Richard and Ronald, wanted more for her children. She turned to the NAACP for help.

On August 18, 1970, the association's general counsel, Nathaniel Jones, filed suit in the federal district court on Bradley's behalf against a number of officials, including Governor William Milliken because, Jones noted, "these children were kept in schools that the Supreme Court said . . . were unconstitutional." City leaders, hoping to have the case withdrawn, devised a number of plans to integrate the K–12 system, but, as the district court noted, each scheme left the schools overwhelmingly segregated and Detroit even blacker than before. The judge therefore ordered a metropolitan Detroit desegregation plan that spread beyond the city's borders.

The suburbs immediately protested.

The US Supreme Court, however, calmed their fears. Just as *Rodriguez* ensured that funding from affluent, overwhelmingly white suburbs would never leak into schools servicing poor children, *Milliken v. Bradley* ensured that white children would not have to attend schools with black children.

To accomplish this feat, the court had to ignore the role the law had played—in residential segregation; white flight; discriminatory public policy that financed, subsidized, and maintained white suburbs; and legislation that drew and redrew boundaries and curtailed transportation options—in keeping black children trapped in impoverished cities and subpar schools.

Five justices held there was no evidence whatsoever that suburban school districts had discriminated against blacks or been responsible for the racially distinct condition of inner-city Detroit. And if the suburbs were not part of the problem, the court reasoned, they could not be part of the solution. Then, as if to underscore the full retreat from *Brown*, the justices emphasized the importance of "local control" of schools and chastised the district court for overstepping its bounds. What's more, they added that *Brown* did not require "any particular racial balance in each school, grade, or classroom."

Justice Marshall's dissent was a roaring eulogy to a once-promising landmark decision. He was astounded at the majority's "superficial" reasoning that had now resulted in the "emasculation of our constitutional guarantee of equal protection."

Marshall balked at the notion of suburban innocence. He scoffed at the idea that the Detroit public schools were locally controlled. The State of Michigan, he said, devised, tweaked, contorted, and, in fact, ran the K–12 system. Michigan, then, had the power to consolidate school districts but chose time and time again to keep white suburban ones separate and distinct from those in the city.

What's more, Marshall pointed out, in 1980 when the city tried to exert some authority to implement *Brown* by redrawing school boundaries, the state legislature crushed Detroit's efforts. And there was this: the same law that allowed Michigan to fund school buses in suburban schools banned the use of state transportation funds for students in the city of Detroit. This, Marshall noted, led to the "construction of small walk-in neighborhood schools, . . . which reflected, to the greatest extent feasible, extensive residential segregation."

How the justices, given this firmly documented track record of discrimination, could absolve the state from responsibility for the racially divided metropolitan school system it created, Marshall had no idea: it "simply flies in the face of reality." For Marshall, the court's decision wasn't about "the neutral principle of law," but about white public sentiment that, "we have gone far enough in enforcing the Constitution's guarantee of equal justice."

As black access to quality public schools drifted farther and farther away, entrance into colleges and universities became even more difficult as well—thanks in no small part to the US Supreme Court's 1978 *Bakke* decision.

Allan Bakke, a thirty-five-year-old white man, had applied to the University of California, Davis, medical school and been turned down twice. Bakke sued, arguing that the university's quota system allowed the admission of blacks and Latinos who had lower Medical College Admission Test, or MCAT, scores than his.

There were, of course, whites who had also gained entry into the medical school program with scores lower than Bakke's, but their entrance was not the focus of his suit. Nor was the tendency of the medical school's dean to guarantee admission to a number of his friends' and political allies' children (despite their lack of qualifications). Admissions based on alumni connections and high-level friendships, while generally dovetailing with whiteness, were not explicitly based on race and therefore not subject to "strict scrutiny." Instead, the university's policy to admit sixteen blacks and Latinos in a class of one hundred, Bakke charged, had denied him equal protection under the law.

In the highly contentious and fractious decision, the court narrowly came down on Allan Bakke's side on June 26, 1978. The five justices who agreed with Bakke asserted that they would only countenance the use of race in admissions for well-defined diversity purposes, while preferring the broader, more multicultural scope of "disadvantaged," which would, for example, recognize what a "farm boy from Idaho" could bring to Harvard. These justices were also concerned about the "reverse discrimination" heaped on whites applying to colleges and universities who, as William Bowen and Derek Bok put it in *The Shape of the River*, "bore no responsibility for any wrongs suffered by minorities." As for admissions policies designed to atone for past discrimination against minorities, John F. Kennedy appointee Justice Byron White was unequivocal: "I do not accept that position."

Attempting to observe the law while also living up to an ethos they had now taken to heart, universities frantically turned to vaguer notions of "diversity," but the definition of that word soon became so expansive that by the twenty-first century white males would actually be the primary beneficiaries of Affirmative Action in college admissions.

Even as the court rejected history, Thurgood Marshall's dissent in *Bakke* recounted 350 years of "the most pervasive and ingenious forms of racial discrimination" against black people. He then expressed disbelief that the court would deny California the right to apply a remedy in the face of that kind of sordid history.

Astounded as Marshall may have been, viewed through a different lens, the court's decision made calculated sense. Black Americans had rushed right through the barely opened door of opportunity pushed ajar by the Civil Rights Movement: from 1970 to 1978, the number of blacks enrolled in college had literally doubled. And in just a little more than a decade, the percentage of black Americans who had a college degree climbed to 6 percent from 4 percent.

This occurred through a combination of black determination and aspiration coupled with the protections of Affirmative Action (where schools actively sought black students rather than shut them out) and federal student financial aid (which helped defray tuition costs for a people overwhelmingly impoverished). All this had significantly changed the game. Nixon's policies and the US Supreme Court choices had set the stage for the reversal of black gains.

Much of this reversal, though, would not be carried out until after Nixon's presidency.

Ronald Reagan used coded language to roll back progress made through the Civil Rights Act and the Voting Rights Act. Without uttering words that explicitly referred to race, Reagan painted vivid pictures of racial entitlement, and his ruthless budget cuts disproportionately affected black citizens.

17

THE REAGAN REVOLUTION

HAILED AS ONE OF THE MOST POPULAR AND even greatest presidents, Ronald Reagan oversaw the rollback of many of the gains black people had achieved through the Civil Rights Movement. Between the time that he took the oath of office in 1981 and the waning days of his second term in 1988, conditions regressed to levels reminiscent of the early 1960s.

Journalist Hodding Carter described Reagan as "part George Wallace and part Nixon and a more effective southern strategist than both put together." Reagan's aura of sincerity and "aw shucks" geniality lent a welcoming, friendly face to any harshness of the Southern Strategy—something that neither Nixon's brooding ways nor Wallace's angry countenance had ever been able to convey.

Ronald Reagan positively oozed racial innocence in his declaration of fealty to states' rights at the all-white 1980 Neshoba County Fair in Mississippi, which took place not far from the triple murder of civil rights workers Chaney, Goodman, and Schwerner.

In a 1981 interview, Republican consultant Lee Atwater explained the inner logic of, as one commentator termed it, "racism with plausible deniability." Atwater pointed out that back in 1954, politicians could spew the N-word left and right. "By 1968, you can't say '[the N-word]'—that hurts you. Backfires. So you say stuff like forced busing, states' rights and all that stuff. You're getting so abstract now you're talking about cutting taxes, and all these things you're talking about are totally economic things and a byproduct of them is blacks get hurt worse than whites. And subconsciously maybe that is part of it. I'm not saying that," he then deflected.

Reagan was a master of racism with plausible deniability. It was a role tailor-made for the former Hollywood actor.

Reagan cast himself as a traditional conservative, but his disdain for supposed big government was geared not so much toward President Franklin Roosevelt's New Deal programs that had provided paid employment to millions of out-of-work Americans like his father; or social security, which had overwhelmingly benefited whites during the Great Depression. What President Reagan loathed was the Great Society, despite its dispersal of benefits to middle-class whites and its effectiveness in lifting the elderly out of poverty. Reagan succeeded in coding the Great Society as a give-away program for blacks.

Reagan breezily shared anecdotes about how Lyndon Johnson's Great Society handed over hard-earned taxpayer dollars to a "slum dweller" to live in posh government-subsidized housing. Those taxpayer dollars, Reagan alleged, also provided food stamps for one "strapping young buck" to buy steak, while another used the change he received from purchasing an orange to pay for a bottle of vodka. Reagan ridiculed Medicaid recipients as "a faceless mass, waiting for handouts." The imagery was, by design, galling, and although the stories were far from the truth, they succeeded in tapping into a river of widespread white resentment.

Reagan's budget priorities reflected his contempt for the Great Society. He ordered a scorched-earth policy through the programs from education to housing to employment. And he targeted very specifically those programs in which blacks were overrepresented even as he protected the other portions of the social safety net. Take social security, where black people were but a small fraction of the recipients. Reagan kept his hands off social security.

Now take higher education. Almost five times as many black college-bound high school seniors as white came from families with incomes below twelve thousand dollars. Reagan's administration reconfigured various grants and loan packages so that "the needier the student, the harder he or she would be hit by Reagan's student-aid cuts."

Nationwide black college enrollment plummeted from 34 percent to 26 percent. Just at the moment when the postindustrial economy made an undergraduate degree more important than ever, fifteen thousand fewer young black men and women were in college during the early 1980s than had been enrolled in the mid-1970s (although the high school graduation numbers were by now significantly higher).

The plunge in undergraduate enrollment—which no other

racial or ethnic group suffered during this time—cascaded into a substantial decline in the number of black Americans in graduate programs as well.

While access to higher education was tightening, the Reagan administration established enormous roadblocks to quality K–12 public schools for America's black children. The president cavalierly stated that he was "under the impression that the problem of segregated schools has been settled."

The assistant attorney general for civil rights, William Bradford Reynolds, agreed. When Reynolds learned of an effort in South Carolina to dismantle what amounted to Jim Crow education, he was determined that black parents, whom he referred to disparagingly, would have to "jump through every hoop" to file a lawsuit to desegregate the public schools in Charleston. "We are not going to compel children who don't choose to have an integrated education to have one," Reynolds insisted.

Under Reynolds and Attorney General Edwin Meese, the Department of Justice used virtually every legal strategy to dismantle, obstruct, and undermine the only remaining alternative to integrate schools—busing. This included torpedoing a plan to finally desegregate a school district in Louisiana that had openly fought *Brown* since 1956.

Already between a rock and a hard place as result of the US Supreme Court's *Milliken* and *Rodriguez* decisions, black children's passage through the education system became even more difficult during the Reagan years. The Detroit decision meant that children were, for the most part, locked inside their cities and their neighborhoods. *Rodriguez* meant that those city and neighborhood schools would remain or become even more impoverished.

During the Reagan administration the Department of Justice seemed determined to advocate segregated schools as a "remedy," putting its considerable weight on the side of the status quo of inequality. Moreover, the Reagan administration exacerbated that inequality even further as it shredded the safety net.

Not even school lunch programs, geared toward those in greatest economic need, were sacred. As the *Christian Science Monitor* reported, in 1981, they came under attack when "President Reagan trimmed $1.46 billion from $5.66 billion earmarked for child nutrition programs."

He also leveled a double-digit cut for a program designed to provide educational support for poor children in the classroom. This occurred at the very moment when the share of black youth living below the poverty line had increased to almost 43 percent.

The 1980s revealed just how fragile the economic recovery of black Americans was in the wake of 350 years of slavery and Jim Crow. From the 1960s to the 1970s, the black unemployment rate had declined, and the gap between black and white unemployment rates had actually narrowed. By the time Reagan's policies had taken effect, the black unemployment rate had increased and the unemployment gap between blacks and whites had widened to unprecedented levels.

During the early 1980s, the overall black unemployment rate stood at 15.5 percent—"an all-time high" since the Great Depression—while unemployment among black youth was a staggering 45.7 percent. At this point Reagan chose to slash the training, employment, and labor services budget by 70 percent—a cut of $3.805 billion. The only "'urban' program that survived the cuts was federal aid for highways—which primarily benefited suburbs, not cities," said Peter Dreier in "Reagan's Legacy: Homelessness in America."

In keeping with Lee Atwater's mantra that "blacks get hurt worse than whites," Reagan gutted aid to cities so extensively that federal dollars were reduced from 22 percent of a city's budget to 6 percent. This huge loss of federal dollars forced cities to take sharp austerity measures. They shut down libraries, closed municipal hospitals, and cut back on garbage pickup. Some cities even dismantled their police and fire departments.

Reagan further destabilized the economic foundation for black Americans on the job front.

Black men and women are disproportionately employed by the government, in large part because the public sector suffers demonstrably less discrimination in hiring and compensation than private industry. More than 50 percent of the growth in employment for black workers in the United States between 1960 to 1976 was in the public sector. But that avenue into economic stability, even for the college educated, was now threatened by two key developments.

First, the federal government's layoffs were concentrated in the social service agencies, where many black people worked. Reagan had exempted the Department of Defense, for example, while a spokesperson made it clear that, "other divisions of Government would be hit especially hard by the employment reductions." When one agency was abolished in 1981, jobs for nine hundred workers—60 percent of them black—were wiped out. Of the six thousand job cuts scheduled for 1982, nearly half were in the Department of Health and Human Services, a major agency for black employment.

The second development assaulting the job security of black workers was the administration's making utterly ineffective the Equal Employment Opportunity Commission (EEOC), the federal watchdog for employment discrimination.

Reagan did this by appointing inadequate and often incompetent leadership. He was especially keen to select black people, such as future Supreme Court justice Clarence Thomas, who believed there was no group discrimination against people of color or women, certainly nothing that would warrant class-action lawsuits. Under this type of management, the EEOC slowed its investigation and processing of complaints to a crawl. The result was a growing backlog whose legal shelf life expired before the EEOC even got around to investigating. The watchdog had been effectively muzzled.

With the rollback now in full force, the "civil rights gains of the past," remarked Vernon Jordan, then president of the National Urban League, were "now under attack and in danger."

The median family income for black Americans had been higher in the 1970s than it was under Reagan, even as the white median income continued to grow. As a result, black peoples' spending power decreased while that of whites rose, increasing the gap by 12 percent.

In the late 1980s black Harvard-trained economist David Swinton lamented that "in virtually every area of life that counts, black people made strong progress in the 1960s, peaked in the 70s, and have been sliding back ever since."

The Reagan administration ensured it. Indeed, by 1990, blacks in the bottom 20 percent were poorer in relation to whites than at any time since the 1950s. Not surprisingly, the National Urban League labeled the president's policies "a failure" that had "usher[ed] in a new era of stagnation and decline" for the "vast majority of average black Americans."

Reagan's job cuts, retooling of student financial aid to eliminate those most in need, and decimation of antipoverty and social welfare programs "virtually ensured that the goal of the African American community for economic stability and progress would crumble and fade," said Hanes Walton Jr. in his 1997 book, *African American Power and Politics*.

And let us not forget the damage done by the War on Drugs.

Lieutenant Colonel Oliver North was instrumental in ensuring that Contras had the weapons they needed, that money was filtered to arms dealers, and that American federal officials avoided pursuing narcotics cases. This government-sanctioned drug trafficking occurred at the same time that media reported on the epidemic of crack cocaine, especially focusing on black communities.

18

CRACK

"MY FELLOW AMERICANS, THOSE OF YOU WHO tuned in a few weeks ago may remember that the topic of my broadcast was crime," said President Ronald Reagan in a gripping radio address on October 2, 1982. "Well, this week I'd like to narrow that subject down to drugs, an especially vicious virus of crime."

A scourge was upon the land! Hardest hit, the president conveyed, was the "garden spot" of South Florida, which had "turned into a battlefield for competing drug pushers who were terrorizing Florida's citizens."

The president then laid out a potent multiagency strategy using military intelligence and radar to home in on drug traffickers and execute interdiction strikes "to cut off drugs before they left other countries' borders."

There was just one problem.

There was no drug crisis in 1982.

Marijuana use was down. The use of heroin and hallucinogens such as LSD had leveled off. Even first-time cocaine use was bottoming out. So what was the president talking about?

Reagan knew that a drug scourge was certainly coming. Members of the Central Intelligence Agency (CIA), the civilian foreign intelligence service, and of the National Security Council (NSC), the agency responsible for advising the president on foreign policy along with national security, had set things in motion for a plague that would devastate predominantly black South Central Los Angeles and then radiate out to black communities across the United States.

This was all rooted in events that occurred in the Central American nation of Nicaragua.

In 1979, after a coalition of moderate and left-wing Nicaraguans overthrew ruthless dictator and longtime US ally Anastasio Somoza Debayle, the socialist Sandinista National Liberation Front—the Sandinistas—came to power.

Ronald Reagan did not like that. In his mind, this was not a homegrown revolution resulting from years of torture of Nicaraguans and other human rights violations, along with intolerable conditions stemming from rampant greed during the forty years that the Somoza family ruled the country. No, Reagan was sure that the Sandinistas were no more than stooges of the United States of America's archenemy, the Soviet Union, seeking to foment revolution in America's backyard.

The Sandinistas had to be put down.

Shortly after Reagan took the oath of office on January 20, 1981, he ordered CIA director William Casey to do whatever it took to support a small band of anti-Sandinista guerrillas, the *contrarevolucionarios* or the Contras. Most of them were strays from Somoza's feared and hated National Guard.

Later that year, on November 23, 1981, Reagan authorized the CIA to give the Contras even more help. This directive came with a budget of $19.3 million.

But that was not enough, argued the Contras' founder, Enrique Bermúdez. His men needed much more.

So in December 1981, "Reagan signed a secret order authorizing Contra aid for the purpose of deposing the Sandinistas," wrote Michael Schaller in *Ronald Reagan*. But where would the money come from? The CIA and NSC could tap into their budgets just so much. Congress, meanwhile, already stung by the debacle of the Vietnam War, from which the United States finally withdrew in 1973 after nearly ten years of boots on the ground at an economic cost of $2.19 trillion, in 2016 dollars, was not about to loosen the purse strings. And so, at a December 1981 meeting at the Balmoral Hotel in San Jose, Costa Rica, Contra leaders, whom Reagan referred to as the "moral equivalent of the Founding Fathers," floated the idea of trafficking cocaine into California to get the money needed to train and arm the counterrevolutionaries.

With most of the network already established, the plan was rather straightforward. There were the Medellín and Cali cartels in Colombia, South America, to supply the cocaine. President Manuel Noriega's Panama (north of Colombia) had airports for use and money-laundering schemes. The well-known lack of radar detection made landing strips in Costa Rica (north of Panama) prime transport depots. El Salvador's Ilopango air base outside San Salvador could warehouse weapons and drugs.

With the CIA and the NSC ready to keep at bay the FBI, the US Customs Service, and the Drug Enforcement Administration (DEA), flooding the States with cocaine would be a piece of cake.

Initially, Nicaraguan nationals Oscar Danilo Blandón and Norwin Meneses, whose nickname was El Rey de las Drogas (the King of Drugs), set up their wholesale operations in San Francisco. To get the drugs out onto the streets they linked up with Rick "Freeway" Ross, an illiterate yet entrepreneurial black man who became the conduit between the Contra drug runners and the Crips and Bloods gangs in L.A.

The result was nothing less than explosive. From the Contra wholesalers, top-quality cocaine was packaged and sold in little rocks of crack that reaped more than $230,000 per kilo in retail profit. Now, drug money, and all its attendant violence, pounded on a population with double-digit unemployment and declining real wages. The logistical strength of the Bloods and Crips, with an estimated fifty thousand gang members, spread the pain as they set up drug franchises throughout the United States to sell crack like it was on the dollar menu. Soon crack was everywhere, kicking the legs out from under black neighborhoods.

While the government-engineered drug crisis threatened the security of millions of black people, the administration focused on getting the Contras more and more weapons with off-the-books money. In 1982, Reagan's vice president, George H. W. Bush (a former director of the CIA), and his national security adviser, Donald Gregg (a former CIA agent), worked with CIA Director Casey to run a program named Black Eagle to funnel weapons to the Contras. Through a series of top-secret negotiations, US officials worked out landing rights at Panamanian airfields for the

Black Eagle planes to transport weapons to the Contras and the use of Panamanian companies to launder money.

Noriega, who was already in a four-hundred-million-dollar partnership with the Medellín cartel, seized on the profitability of this deal with the White House and began to divert Black Eagle planes and pilots from weapons-running flights to drug-running flights to the southern United States.

The Reagan administration's response?

It simply required the Panamanian president to use a percentage of his drug profits to buy additional weapons for the Contras.

Thus, although Reagan bragged to the American public about using US military resources "to cut off drugs before they left other countries' borders," his staff's shielding of Noriega and the Colombian traffickers actively allowed cocaine imports to the United States to skyrocket by 50 percent within three years. The Medellín cartel's cut alone was ten billion dollars a year in sales.

The Reagan administration's protection of drug traffickers escalated further when the CIA received approval from the Department of Justice in 1982 to remain silent about any key agency "assets" who were involved in the manufacturing, transportation, or sale of narcotics.

Protection for major drug traffickers swung into full gear once Congress, through a series of amendments in 1982 and 1984, shut off all funds to the Contras and banned US material-and-financial support for the overthrow of the government in Nicaragua. Undeterred, the Reagan administration simply ramped up the alternate and illegal streams of revenue it had already devised: drug profits and secret arms sales to Iran, which was under an arms embargo.

At this point Lieutenant Colonel Oliver North, deputy director of the NSC, stepped in to create the larger, more dynamic operation that would soon replace Bush's Black Eagle.

Oliver North brought to the work both a military efficiency and a truly amoral focus. Years later, when under congressional klieg lights, he seemed to imply that the breaking of laws was appropriate. "I remain convinced that what we tried to accomplish was worth the risk," he said during the 1987 Iran-Contra hearings. North understood that his role, working with his CIA counterpart Duane Clarridge, was to ensure that the Contras had weapons. Congress had cut off all funding, so money had to come from somewhere.

That warped framing of the Contras' needs led North to facilitate the trafficking of cocaine into the United States, which included working with the CIA to transport 1,500 kilos of drugs from Bolivia, diverting hundreds of thousands of dollars in humanitarian aid to indicted narcotics traffickers, and refusing to pass the names of known drug runners on to the appropriate authorities.

North also saw to it that the millions of dollars in profits from the sale of narcotics were then funneled to arms dealers, especially in El Salvador and Honduras, who could equip the Contras with everything from boots to grenades.

The FBI learned that under the pretext of "national security," North's NSC routinely intimidated Customs and DEA officials to back off from making good narcotics cases. Moreover, Blandón and Meneses, who trafficked at least five tons of cocaine, or the equivalent of 16.2 million rocks of crack, into California, "led a charmed life" as the NSC and CIA blocked police, sheriffs, and the DEA from stopping the flow of drugs and money.

North even swooped in to rescue a major Contra ally who was arrested by the FBI with 345 kilos of cocaine. Using the full authority and aura of the NSC, North weighed in on the court. The drug kingpin's sentence was reduced by 75 percent (down to five years) and his locale of incarceration changed from a maximum-security to a minimum-security ("Club Fed") facility.

Hand in hand with the inordinate concern about avoiding prison sentences and the legal consequences for those who poured tons of cocaine into the United States, there was an equal determination to lock up and imprison people in the communities bearing the brunt of the White House's narco-funding scheme.

Reagan's speeches and policies focused on enforcement, criminals, and harsh, no-mercy punishment. With the onset of the epidemic of crack, a drug that had become thoroughly associated with black people, notions of treatment went out the window. This despite numerous studies proving that treatment was not only more effective but less costly than incarceration. As a DEA agent would later remark, "no one has yet demonstrated that enforcement will ever win the war on drugs." Nonetheless, Reagan dragged America down the road of mass incarceration.

The decision to fund the Contras with profits from the sale of cocaine, for example, came at a time when the economic downturn had created high unemployment, increasing homelessness, the depletion of savings, and other major stressors, which only heightened the possibility of creating a drug-addicted society at the very moment when narcotics use had actually stabilized or decreased.

As the horrific toll crack cocaine took on lives became more and more obvious, the administration's response was not to fund treatment facilities but to demonize and criminalize black people and provide the federal resources to make incarceration the norm.

"Drugs are menacing our society," President Reagan told the nation in a September 1986 speech delivered from the White House. "They're threatening our values and undercutting our institutions. They're killing our children." This was a nation under attack, said the president in so many words.

"Despite our best efforts," Reagan added with a hint of shock and dismay, "illegal cocaine is coming into our country at alarming levels." At that point, Reagan identified as public enemy number one: "crack."

In this speech, the president not only laid out an epic tale of good, freedom-loving Americans locked in a mortal battle for the nation's soul against crack addicts and drug dealers, but in doing so, he also defined the racial contours of this war.

Media fanned the flames, and then some. With little to no evidence, news outlets warned that crack, reputedly the most addictive drug known to mankind, was galloping out of the crime-filled inner cities and, as *Newsweek* claimed, "rapidly spreading into the suburbs."

The *New York Times* echoed the refrain, identifying "epidemic" crack use from Long Island to "the wealthiest suburbs of Westchester County."

The media's overwhelming tendency to blacken crack only

added to this national panic. Between 1986 and 1987, 76 percent of the articles in the *New York Times*, the *Chicago Tribune*, the *Washington Post*, and the *Los Angeles Times* dealing with crack referenced black Americans either directly or through code words such as "urban" and "inner city." Whites were mentioned only one-third of the time. The message was clear: the black "plague" was coming.

The crack plague had already swept through black neighborhoods around the country with absolutely no warning. There had been minor use of crack in the 1970s, but it began to show up visibly in 1984 and exploded in 1985 and 1986—just as Congress cut off funding to the Contras, leaving the administration desperate to finance the war against the Sandinistas.

As battles over lucrative drug turf escalated, black communities were besieged with rampant gang violence. Most had no idea how this crack scourge had arisen or how those who had once toted simple handguns now carried AK-47s and other semiautomatic, military-grade weapons. But no one was confused about the horrific consequences.

In 1988, a National Urban League report declared that the "gains made over the past 25 years, many the result of the Civil Rights Movement in the 1960s, will . . . unravel unless steps are taken to arrest the pervasive problem of crime in the black community."

A research team from Harvard and the University of Chicago explained, "Between 1984 and 1994, the homicide rate for Black males aged 14–17 more than doubled and homicide rates for Black males aged 18–24 increased almost as much."

The magnitude of the firepower and the sheer number of

killings were critical factors that led black life expectancy rates to decline—something that not even slavery or Jim Crow had been able to accomplish. And there was the collateral damage: babies dying in the womb, low-birth-weight babies, and boys and girls put in foster care.

Researchers concluded that the perilous decline of black Americans on so many quality-of-life indicators "represents a break from decades of convergence between Blacks and Whites on many of these measures."

And the situation for blacks was about to get exponentially worse.

In 1986, Congress passed the Anti-Drug Abuse Act. It called for mandatory sentencing. It emphasized punishment over treatment. It created the 100-to-1 difference in sentencing between possession of *crack* and possession of *powder cocaine* based on the myth that the cheap narcotic rock was more addictive than its powder form.

The NAACP explained the law's 100-to-1 formulation thusly: "a person must possess 500 grams of powder cocaine before they are subject to the same mandatory prison sentence (5 years) as an individual who is convicted of possessing just 5 grams of crack cocaine (despite the fact that pharmacologically, these two drugs are identical)."

Tougher sentencing policies were not the answer, said the National Urban League. The incarceration rate would be so high, it warned, that society would not be able to bear the costs. Congress, nonetheless, followed up in 1988 with an even harsher version of the Anti-Drug Abuse Act that instituted mandatory

SUPREME MOVES

The US Supreme Court . . .

• affirmed that police, even though their overall racial bias is well documented, can stop anyone based on something far below the understood threshold of probable cause (*Terry v. Ohio*, 1968);

• approved racial profiling (*United States v. Brignoni-Ponce*, 1975);

• upheld harsh mandatory sentencing for drug offenses (*Hutto v. Davis*, 1982);

• tossed out irrefutable evidence of racial bias in sentencing because of its implications for the entire criminal justice system and required, instead, proof of overt, visible discrimination against the individual defendant to support a claim of violation of equal protection under the law (*McClesky v. Kemp*, 1987);

• approved, as the justices openly admitted, "ridiculous" peremptory strikes to eliminate blacks from a jury so long as the prosecutor's stated rationale was not based on race (*Purkett v. Elem*, 1995);

• shielded district attorneys from disclosing the role the defendant's race played in prosecutorial discretion (*Armstrong v. United States*, 1996);

• ruled that police could use their discretion instead of probable cause to search motorists for drugs (*Whren v. United States*, 1996);

• determined that Title VI of the Civil Rights Act cannot be used by private individuals to sue entities, such as prosecutors or police, in the criminal justice system on grounds of racial bias (*Alexander v. Sandoval*, 2001); and

• found that pretext traffic stops—for example, having a busted taillight or not using a turn signal—are a legal and permissible ruse for police to hunt for drugs (*Atwater v. City of Lago Vista*, 2001).

sentencing for even a first-time offense, and added the death penalty for certain crimes, including homicide, that involved drugs. It also denied housing and other human rights to those whose greatest crime was having a friend or a family member in the drug trade pay a visit.

The US Supreme Court had played a critical role in tightening the noose. A series of cases, beginning in 1968 but escalating dramatically during the tenure of Warren Burger, then William Rehnquist as Chief Justice (1969–1986 and 1986–2005, respectively), legalized racial discrimination in the criminal justice system.

Residents of Tulia, Texas, rally in support of black citizens arrested in a 1999 massive drug bust. As the accused citizens' cases came to trial, it became clear that there was insufficient evidence to link these citizens to the crime and that racial biases had played a large role in their arrests.

"STREETS CLEARED
OF GARBAGE"

TAKEN TOGETHER, THE US SUPREME COURT
rulings listed in the previous chapter allowed, indeed encouraged, the criminal justice system to run racially amok. And that's exactly what happened on July 23, 1999, in a small Southern town of a few thousand souls and with a tiny black population: Tulia, Texas, in the Texas Panhandle.

In the dead of night, local police launched a massive raid and busted a major cocaine trafficking ring in Tulia. At least that's how it was billed by the local media. Having been tipped off about the bust, members of the media lined up to get the best, most humiliating photographs of forty-six of the town's residents, handcuffed, in pajamas, underwear, and uncombed bed hair, being paraded into the jail for booking.

The *Tulia Sentinel* later ran a front-page story on the raid under the headline TULIA'S STREETS CLEARED OF GARBAGE.

Forty of those arrestees were black. Of the six whites and Latinos who were arrested in the raid, all had relations—familial or friendly—with Tulia's black community.

The raid was the result of an eighteen-month investigation by Tom Coleman, soon to be named Texas Lawman of the Year.

Attached to the federally funded Panhandle Regional Narcotics Task Force, based in Amarillo, about fifty miles away from Tulia, Tom Coleman didn't lead a team of investigators. Instead, he single-handedly identified each member of this massive cocaine operation and made more than one hundred undercover drug purchases. Coleman's testimony immediately led to the conviction of thirty-eight of the forty-six people arrested on the night of July 23.

Joe Moore, a sixty-year-old pig farmer, for example, was sentenced to 99 years for selling two hundred dollars' worth of cocaine to Coleman. Kizzie White was hit with twenty-five years, while William "Cash" Love, a white man who had fathered White's youngest child, landed 434 years for possessing an ounce of cocaine.

Other cases were just waiting to get into the clogged court system.

Things began to unravel, however, when Kizzie White's sister, Tonya, went to trial. Coleman swore that she had sold him drugs. Tonya, however, had video proof that she was at a bank in Oklahoma City—three hundred miles away—cashing a check at the very moment Coleman claimed to have bought cocaine from her.

Another defendant, Billy Don Wafer, had time sheets and his

boss's eyewitness testimony that he was at work and not out sell-ing drugs to Coleman when the officer said he was.

Coleman also swore under oath that he had purchased cocaine from Yul Bryant, a tall bushy-haired man, only to have Bryant—bald and five feet six—appear in court. It became clear that something was terribly awry.

Officer Coleman, in fact, had no proof whatsoever that any of the alleged drug deals had taken place. There were no audio-tapes. No photographs. No witnesses. No other police officers present. No fingerprints but his on the bags of drugs. No records. He claimed to have written each drug transaction on his leg but then washed away the evidence accidentally when he showered.

Additional investigation led to no corroborating proof of Coleman's allegations. What's more, when the police arrested those forty-six people and vigorously searched their homes and possessions, they found no drugs or drug paraphernalia, no weapons, no stockpile of cash, or anything else to indicate that a pig farmer, a housewife, or anyone else arrested was actually a drug kingpin.

What was discovered was judicial misconduct running ram-pant in the war on drugs in Tulia, Texas. A war with a clear racial bias.

Coleman perjured himself on the stand when he claimed to be an upstanding, law-abiding citizen. In fact, he was under indictment for theft in his previous position as a deputy sheriff in another county.

The prosecutor, Terry McEachern, knew about this but failed to disclose it to the defense attorneys. The district attorney also ensured that across 96 jurors for all trials, only one was black.

Moreover, Judge Edward Self, who presided over the lion's share of the trials, publicly expressed his support for the prosecutors and sealed Coleman's employment records, including that charge of embezzlement as a deputy sheriff.

Although the white community consistently denied that race played any role in this, the speed and efficiency in which the criminal justice system worked to sentence black defendants and their white and Latino friends to decades in prison, based solely on the unsubstantiated testimony of a man under indictment, suggests otherwise.

Randy Credico of the William Moses Kunstler Fund for Racial Justice, called Tulia "a mass lynching . . . It's like being accused of raping someone in Indiana in the 1930s. You didn't do it, but it doesn't matter because a bunch of Klansmen on the jury are going to string you up anyway."

But this was not the 1930s. This was the beginning of the twenty-first century, and a powerful Civil Rights Movement had bridged those two eras. Yet now felony convictions, chiefly via the war on drugs, replaced the explicit use of race as the mechanism to deny black Americans their rights as citizens.

Disenfranchisement.

Permanent bans on jury service.

Legal discrimination in employment, housing, and education.

Despite the civil rights legislation of the 1960s, the above are now all burdens carried by those who have been incarcerated for felonies.

That burden has been disproportionately shouldered by the black community. Only 12.3 percent of the nation's population, it makes up 37.9 percent of those incarcerated.

Even more disconcertingly, these felony convictions have had little to do with ensuring the safety and security of the nation and in most cases target the wrong culprits.

Given the poor state of the schools, crushing poverty, and lack of viable living-wage options for large swaths of the black population, black Americans' drug use should mirror their staggering incarceration rates. According to Human Rights Watch, "the proportion of blacks in prison populations exceeds the proportion among state residents in every single state." In Missouri, for example, black Americans make up 11.2 percent of the state's residents but 41.2 percent of those incarcerated. But there is no direct correlation between drug use and incarceration.

Despite all the economic and social pressures they confront, and despite the media narrative and disproportionate policing and sentencing, black people have shown an amazing resilience in the face of drugs. They are among the least likely drug users of all racial and ethnic groups in the United States. Despite all the stereotypes, they are among the least likely to sell drugs, too. As a major study out of the University of Washington revealed, even when confronted with irrefutable evidence of whites' engagement with the illegal-drug trade, law enforcement has continued to focus its efforts on the black population.

Thus, after the Civil Rights Movement, when black Americans were making incredible strides in education, voting, and employment, those gains were a threat to the status quo of inequality.

As Naomi Murakawa wrote in her book *The First Civil Right*, the "United States did not face a crime problem that was racialized; it faced a race problem that was criminalized."

Crowds celebrate President Barack Obama's inauguration in 2009, a landmark moment in US racial history. Some conservative opposition claimed he had won the election via voter fraud, setting off a massive voter disenfranchisement effort.

20

OBAMA

ON NOVEMBER 4, 2008, THE UNITED STATES seemed to be crossing the racial Rubicon: a black man, Barack Hussein Obama, was elected president of the United States.

For a brief moment, the mirage of hope hung in the air, mesmerizing people in the United States and around the world.

In Tehran, capital of Iran, a newspaper's deputy editor proclaimed, "The country that they called 'the great Satan,' [declaring] it the symbol of all kinds of tyranny, has enough respect for democratic values that [it has] allowed a black candidate to come this far and even become a president."

In Moscow, eighteen-year-old Ilya Glazunov called the United States "really majestic. I feel it is a country where everything is possible."

Black South African Nobel Peace Prize winner, former anti-apartheid activist, and former Anglican archbishop Desmond

Tutu agreed. Obama's victory, said Tutu, told "people of color that for them, the sky is the limit."

"HISTORIC WIN" blazed the headline in the *Philadelphia Inquirer* the day after the election.

Not everyone was ecstatic. As the Republican postmortems on the election poured in, it was clear that the voting patterns spelled trouble for the GOP.

Obama had captured a significantly higher share of the white vote than had John Kerry in the 2004 election. What's more, 66 percent of Latinos who voted did so overwhelmingly for Barack Obama, not to mention 62 percent of Asians who voted, 56 percent of women who voted, 66 percent of voters under thirty years of age, and 95 percent of black people who voted.

The last of these was not surprising. What was not anticipated, however, was that for the first time in history, the black voter turnout rate nearly equaled the white voter turnout rate.

The only groups the Republican presidential candidate John McCain could claim to have run away with were elderly white people and white evangelical Christians. And therein lay the problem: those sectors of the American voting population were not growing.

Also distressing for the GOP was this: the largest percentage of eligible voters in forty years had cast a ballot in the 2008 election. This was not only a record turnout. It was one that delivered an 8.5 million vote differential in Obama's favor, with *15 million* new voters overall.

"It's a bad thing for Republicans when you drill down into these states and see lots of new voters, newcomers," groaned Rich Lowry, editor of the conservative magazine *National Review*.

"It's like, where did all the Republicans go? Did they move to Utah?"

This was no idle question. The surge in voters came from all across the racial and ethnic ranks—blacks, Latinos, and Asians—of which only 8 percent identified as Republican. While the number of white people who voted remained roughly the same as it had been in the 2004 election, *two million more* blacks, *two million more* Latinos, and *six hundred thousand more* Asians voted in 2008.

Even more unsettling to the GOP was the youth and relative poverty of first-time voters. Those making less than fifteen thousand dollars a year nearly doubled their turnout to the polls, going from 18 percent in 2004 to 34 percent in 2008. Not surprisingly, these new voters favored the federal government playing a greater role in making education more affordable, in instituting a program to rebuild the nation's infrastructure, and in raising the minimum wage as a start to improving the quality of life for millions of Americans.

Nearly 69 percent of first-time voters had cast their ballots for Obama.

Yes, the GOP was in trouble.

Trapped between a demographically declining support base and an ideological straitjacket that made the party not only unresponsive but also repugnant to millions of Americans, the GOP reached for a tried-and-true weapon: disenfranchisement.

Once it became clear that the voter turnout rate of blacks had nearly equaled that of whites, as Penda Hair of the progressive Advancement Project noted, "Conservatives were looking at it and saying 'We've got to clamp things down.' They'd always tried to suppress the black vote, but it was then that they came up with new schemes." The old schemes involving physical and economic intimidation and violence simply would not fly.

The new schemes veiled the white rage behind a legitimate-sounding concern: protecting the integrity of the ballot box from voter fraud. Paul Weyrich, a conservative activist and the founder of the American Legislative Exchange Council (ALEC), was explicit early in the history of his group: "I don't want everybody to vote." He noted that the GOP's "leverage in the elections quite candidly goes up as the voting populace goes down."

After the 2008 election, ALEC stepped in to draft "model voter-ID legislation . . . that . . . popped up in very similar form in states like Pennsylvania and Texas and Wisconsin," Ari Berman, author of *Give Us the Ballot: The Modern Struggle for Voting Rights in America*, told the *New York Times Magazine* in 2015. As always, the mantra was *Stop voter fraud!*

And the propaganda was this: Obama's victory was not the result of a brilliant strategy that had outmaneuvered the Clinton juggernaut by energizing the youth and the poor to believe that they had an actual stake in America, but rather the Obama win was the sordid outcome of a brazenly stolen election tied directly to all those new voters.

Stop voter fraud!

This charge was in the wake of a Department of Justice study that revealed that out of the 197 million votes cast for federal candidates between 2002 and 2005, a mere 40 people were indicted for voter fraud. Of that number all of 26 convictions or guilty pleas were registered—roughly .00000013 percent of the tallied ballots.

Stop voter fraud!

In 2011, in Wisconsin, a rigorous voter ID law was passed following charges of rampant fraud at the polls. But in a state with more than 3.4 million registered voters, the few people convicted of voter fraud each year were usually ex-felons, who simply sought to cast a ballot before their voting rights had been restored.

Key to the charge that Obama had stolen the election was the Association of Community Organizations for Reform Now (ACORN), a community-based group that had launched extensive voter registration drives throughout the nation.

Even before the first vote was cast, John McCain accused ACORN of "perpetrating one of the greatest frauds in voter history in this country, maybe destroying the fabric of democracy." By the time the election was over, reported *Newsweek*'s Katie Connolly in 2009, "a 52% majority of GOP voters nationally [thought] that ACORN stole the presidential election for Barack Obama . . . with only 27% granting that he won it legitimately."

ACORN was many things, but a well-oiled machine able to pull off nationwide voter fraud it was not. In the 2008 election it was terribly sloppy. It lacked either rigorous oversight or a check-and-balance system for its voter registration hires. ACORN had several employees who wanted a paycheck but who did not want to do the hard work of registering voters. These people faked voter registration cards. The law nonetheless requires that all cards be submitted to local election officials, which meant that even those obviously bogus ones could not be thrown in the trash. Hence, Mickey Mouse apparently wanted to vote, as did Jive Turkey. This debacle was tailor-made to fuel the narrative of widespread voter ID fraud. Stoking the flames further yet was Obama's work, years earlier, with an affiliate of ACORN.

Oddly enough, ACORN had been investigated extensively by the George W. Bush administration, which had pressured US attorneys to find evidence of fraud. No matter how hard they tried, they simply couldn't. And when some of the attorneys in the Department of Justice refused to throw suspicion on Democratic candidates by filing half-baked or trumped-up charges of voter registration fraud, especially before an election, they were summarily fired.

There have been proven instances of voter fraud in the past, but those cases involved election officials' wrongdoing or the manipulation of absentee ballots. The kind of voter registration fraud that seized the imagination of GOP activists—fraud that is based on stealing someone's identity or creating a fake persona to cast a ballot, thus altering the results of an election, is in fact very rare. The convoluted scheme is not used because "it is an exceedingly dumb strategy," explained Richard L. Hasen in his book *The Voting Wars*. To have real impact would require an improbable conspiracy involving millions of people.

Robert Brandon, president of the Fair Elections Legal Network, noted that, "You can't steal an election one person at a time. You can by stuffing ballot boxes—but voter I.D.s won't stop that."

But onward marched the GOP to stop voter fraud.

In the stop-voter-fraud campaign, each restriction and requirement crafted and pushed through Republican-dominated state legislatures and signed off by Republican governors was carefully aimed at the population of voters who had helped put a black

man in the White House. The goal, as one Mitt Romney sup-
porter expressed in 2012 via a T-shirt he wore, was to "Put the
White Back in the White House."

And those efforts turned poor whites, students, and the
elderly into collateral damage that got caught in the blowback.

One of the most burdensome if harmless-sounding changes in
what states require of citizens trying to vote is the government-
issued photo ID. In Texas, that makes more than one million
student IDs ineligible while concealed weapons permits are valid.

The Brennan Center for Justice estimates that as "many as
12 percent of eligible voters nationwide may not have government-
issued photo ID," and that "percentage is likely even higher for
students, seniors and people of color."

In December 2011, a joint report by the NAACP and the
NAACP Legal Defense and Educational Fund emphasized
the "alarming" impact of the law. The ID requirement would
eliminate more than six million black and nearly three million
Latino voters. And while that is roughly 25 percent of black and
16 percent of Latino voters, "only 8% of whites are without a current government-issued photo ID."

So why wouldn't people simply acquire a government-issue
photo ID and get on with it?

It's not that simple.

Georgia's laws, for instance, require *three* separate categories
of documentation to secure a government-issued photo ID. The
first is proof of citizenship, which overwhelmingly requires either
a birth certificate or a passport, but the cost of a passport (which
for the working poor is roughly 10 percent of one month's

take-home pay) puts that out of reach for many. Up to 13 million American citizens do not have ready access to citizenship documents, the Brennan Center reports, and this phenomenon is highly correlated with people of color, the poor, and the elderly, people for whom it is no easy feat to navigate the process of, say, replacing a lost birth certificate, and people who may not even be aware that the cost of a passport card is a lot less than the cost of a passport book.

Second, Georgia requires documentation of the prospective voter's social security number, which is either the social security card itself or a W-2. If you don't have your original social security card, you must provide further identification—again, an expensive passport or the state issued-identification that you are trying to get in the first place—to get a replacement card. A W-2 requires a job of course. In 2011, black unemployment in Georgia was 16.4 percent. In the capital city of Atlanta, nearly one-fourth of all black American adults were unemployed, compared with just 3.1 percent of whites. Access to a W-2, then, bears strong and fairly obvious racial implications.

Finally, Georgia requires for proof of residence two addressed items of mail, generally, a bank statement and a utility bill. More than 20 percent of black Americans, as compared with 3 percent of whites, do not have a bank account.

Also due to the changes in the economy and the need to pool limited resources, almost 6 percent of all families in the United States are in multigenerational households. Black Americans, those younger than thirty-five years old, and Asians and Latinos are overly represented in this type of living arrangement. Regardless of the number of adults in a home, only one name appears on the utility bills, making it difficult for the others to prove they actually live there.

Wisconsin took another tack when Republican governor Scott Walker championed a bill requiring a government-issued photo ID to vote, and then proceeded to close the Department of Motor Vehicles (DMV), where people could obtain a photo ID, in areas with a lot of Democratic voters. At the same time, in Republican strongholds DMV hours were extended. And "this in a state in which half of blacks and Hispanics are estimated to lack a driver's license and a quarter of its DMV offices are open less than one day per month," wrote Jeremiah Goulka in "Are Voter ID Laws a Form of Racism?"

In Texas, there are no ID-issuing offices in fully a third of its counties.

Alabama, while enacting a voter ID law in 2011, subsequently shut down DMV offices in its Black Belt counties, the very ones that overwhelmingly voted for Obama in the 2012 election. Facing a national uproar after announcing the closures, Governor Robert Bentley backtracked, but ever so slightly. Alabama agreed to allow the DMV offices in the Black Belt counties to be open at least one day a month.

The Republicans in Pennsylvania pushed through a rigorous voter ID law and then failed to follow through on a pledge to provide free IDs for those who could not afford them. Nor did Pennsylvania establish enough mobile units to reach residents, particularly those in rural areas. Issuing a stinging rebuke, state judge Bernard McGinley declared that since Pennsylvania required the IDs, it now needed to provide the means for the state's citizens to obtain what had essentially become the passport to the vote. The judge noted the scarcity of mobile units and the fact that many of the license offices were open only a few days a week, which had created lengthy wait times and virtual inaccessibility and, therefore, placed "an unreasonable burden on people trying to exercise their right to vote," wrote Sari Horwitz for the *Washington Post*.

In another ploy toward disenfranchisement, efforts were made to eliminate or greatly curtail early voting.

Early voting is essential for people who cannot take time off from work on a Tuesday to vote. We are talking about men and women with jobs where they must punch the clock, may take no more than an hour for lunch, and who must travel miles to get from where they live or work to their polling place. On Election Day, moreover, the lines at the voting precincts in key neighborhoods have been notoriously long. Six- to twelve-hour waits in line were reported in the 2008 election, and, as a recent Brennan Center study found, predominately black and Latino precincts experienced longer wait times because the government allocated fewer operable machines and staff to those polling places.

Early voting had provided one important and demonstrably successful solution—and that was the problem. Once Florida governor Rick Scott took office in 2011, he and a group of GOP consultants discerned the pathways black Americans used to exercise the right to vote and promptly set out to shut those routes down.

Scott slashed early voting from two weeks to eight days.

Governor Scott also got rid of the opportunity to vote on the Sunday right before Election Day. Statewide in 2008, black people made up more than *one-third* of those who voted on the Sunday before Election Day. And, in Palm Beach County, more than 60 percent of those voting early were black Americans, many of whom had boarded buses right after church to cast their ballots. Eliminating that pathway to the polls was high on the priority hit list. Said one Republican consultant: "I know that the cutting out of the Sunday before Election Day was one of their targets only because that's a big day when the black churches organize themselves."

Another device in the disenfranchisement tool kit was a tactic that William Rehnquist used in Arizona in 1962, several years before Richard Nixon appointed him to the US Supreme Court. First, Rehnquist's group of Republican stalwarts sent "do not forward" mail to residents in Democratic strongholds. Then, based on the faulty premise that returned cards meant the person was no longer in the district, on Election Day his Army of Challengers questioned the legitimacy of the voter based on nothing more substantial than returned mail, and demanded that the mostly black and Latino population prove that they could read and write by interpreting portions of the Constitution. In the run up to the election of 2012, Republican operatives sent out mass mailings to minority neighborhoods, waiting for the "return to sender" cards to come back, then checking those names against public voting rolls in order to demand a purge of those names.

Florida has been one of the most aggressive states to adopt this procedure, using records from the Department of Motor Vehicles to identify and scrub 180,000 names from the voter rolls. More important, it began this purge just months before the upcoming 2012 presidential election, limiting the opportunity for individuals to verify the reliability of the edited list. Voters showed up at the polls only to find that their names were nowhere to be found. They had been disenfranchised. Indeed, after the election, Florida's secretary of state identified only 85 names (out of the original 180,000) that should have been removed from the list.

In the process of whittling down that number, the inherent racial and ethnic bias in the purge became clear. After the first wave of complaints, Florida officials culled the number of "suspect voters" to 2,700. Yet, as a *Miami Herald* analysis cites, eighty-seven percent of the people on the list are minorities, and 58 percent are Hispanic.

Such voter-roll purges were fully supported by the updated version of Rehnquist's Army of Challengers. The modern incarnation, True the Vote, was founded in Texas—born of the Tea Party—and defines itself as a citizen-based group committed to "free and fair elections for all Americans." Using a flawed database and even Facebook, True the Vote members pore over public lists of registered voters, identify those whose names or addresses don't match up perfectly with the group's own records, and then set out to challenge those marked on their list as frauds. They often target the multigenerational households that are more common in black, Latino, and Asian families, arguing that an address with a number of adults who have registered to vote has to be bogus. True the Vote poll watchers have been conspicuously present in black precincts on Election Day, taking notes, ruffling feathers, challenging voters, clogging the lines, causing delays, frustrating voters who then leave without casting a ballot, ignoring warnings from election officials, and looking for any evidence of supposed ACORN-like fraud.

Councilman Ernest Montgomery lost a 2008 election in Shelby County, Alabama, when boundaries were redrawn in his district to exclude a large percentage of black voters. The US Department of Justice ordered that the election be held again with the district's original boundaries, but Shelby County fought the decision at the US Supreme Court and won, resulting in a massive blow to the Voting Rights Act.

21

SHELBY COUNTY V. HOLDER: GUTTING THE VRA

BARACK OBAMA'S ELECTION SPARKED A LEVEL of voter suppression not seen so clearly or disturbingly in decades. Nowhere was this more apparent than in the Supreme Court's 2013 gutting of the Voting Rights Act.

The case began in 2008. Shelby County, Alabama, commissioners annexed several subdivisions to the city of Calera, then redrew the district boundaries of the lone black councilman, Ernest Montgomery. This reduced the percentage of black Americans in his precinct from 69 to 29 percent. Montgomery lost the election.

Mind you, in redrawing the district boundaries Shelby County thumbed its nose at the VRA's Section 5, which required preclearance to make changes to election procedures, voting qualifications, or district boundaries.

Attorneys from the NAACP Legal Defense Fund alerted the Department of Justice to what Shelby County had done. The DOJ, in turn, required Shelby County to hold another election using the original district boundaries. The commissioners balked, asserting that they had made so much progress that oversight was not needed anymore.

In 2010, Shelby County filed suit in federal district court. This lawsuit charged that the VRA's Section 5 was unconstitutional because Congress did not have the authority to reauthorize the act in 2006.

The district court sharply disagreed, as did the US Court of Appeals in 2011. The judges were unequivocal: "Congress drew reasonable conclusions from the extensive evidence it gathered and acted pursuant to the Fourteenth and Fifteenth Amendments, which entrust Congress with ensuring that the right to vote—surely among the most important guarantees of political liberty in the Constitution—is not abridged on account of race. In this context, we owe much deference to the considered judgment of the People's elected representatives."

But then came US Supreme Court's earth-quaking 2013 decision in *Shelby County v. Holder,* with "Holder" being DOJ chief Eric Holder Jr., President Obama's pick for US Attorney General, the first time a black person would hold this position.

The High Court looked at Shelby County's clear violation of the law and came down squarely on the side of the commissioners in a 5–4 decision. Chief Justice John Roberts and four other justices considered the rationale for the Voting Rights Act obsolete. They conceded the past terror and the evil laws that had resulted in millions of black Americans being disenfranchised. But it was a new day in the South, Roberts wrote confidently in the majority opinion. "Largely because of the Voting Rights Act, voting tests were abolished, disparities in voter registration and turnout due to race were erased, and African Americans attained political office in record numbers."

That success should have led the court to conclude that, without the VRA's protection, those changes could easily be erased. Instead the VRA's success led Roberts and associate justices Antonin Scalia, Anthony Kennedy, Samuel Alito, and the lone black US Supreme Court justice, Clarence Thomas, to veer in the opposite direction. They asserted that because the law had worked so well, and because other states were not held to the same scrutiny, the act, as reauthorized by Congress in 2006, was out of sync with modern times. With that, the justices kept Section 5 but declared unconstitutional Section 4 of the act, which provides the conditions under which the Department of Justice may place a jurisdiction under the oversight stipulated by the statute.

How the court arrived at that decision is a testament to twisted facts and ignored evidence. Roberts, for example, contended that the VRA placed burdens on localities because of past misdeeds that could not be justified by "current needs." However, the so-called burdens Roberts alluded to had been placed only on those jurisdictions with a long, well-documented history of discrimination and a systematic pattern, after the initial passage of the Voting Rights Act in 1965, of trying to craft laws that violated the basic right to vote for all citizens.

What's more, the VRA contains a "bail out" provision: that is, an exemption from federal government monitoring for jurisdictions that behaved themselves when it came to peoples' voting rights for a period of at least five years. Numerous counties in

Virginia, as well as North Carolina's Wake County, Georgia's Sandy Springs, Texas's North Austin, and Alabama's Pinson, having met the standard, have been thus "bailed out." The fact that the majority of other locales in the old Confederacy, which are now in the heart of GOP country, have not been bailed out says more about the state of the right to vote in those places than it does about the rigors of the Voting Rights Act.

Moreover, the court's depiction of the VRA as static and unduly discriminatory against the South is wrong on both counts. First, over the years the DOJ has had to *"bail in"*—that is, put under scrutiny—other districts throughout the United States because of racially discriminatory laws and policies that have blocked equal access to the ballot box. The places bailed in include eight counties in Arizona, one in Idaho, four jurisdictions in Alaska, two in California, three counties in New York, and one in Wyoming, as well as towns in Connecticut, Massachusetts, Maine, and New Hampshire.

Discrimination has never been just a Southern phenomenon, and the VRA has recognized that. In short, the vigorous use of bail-in and bail-out provisions seriously weakens Roberts's argument that the law is an ancient artifact that does not address "current needs." Moreover, the court's overriding concern that the law is somehow anti-South willfully overlooks the region's continuing attempts to snuff out black votes.

Discrimination did not stop in 1965, nor in 1975, nor in 2005. According to the NAACP, since 2011, nine out of the eleven states of the old Confederacy have adopted or proposed two or more requirements to tighten access to the polls. These tactics included placing restrictions on voter registration drives and requiring a government-issued photo ID to vote. The only thing that kept the wolves at bay during that time was the Voting Rights Act's pre-clearance provision. The US Supreme Court's ruling in *Shelby County v. Holder* turned the dogs loose.

Immediately following the ruling, Arizona, Arkansas, Florida, Iowa, Kansas, Mississippi, North Carolina, Texas, and Virginia all passed a series of voter suppression laws. Then, right before the 2014 midterm elections, thirteen additional states passed voter restriction statutes. All were under the guise of protecting the "integrity" of the ballot box, but all had the intent of limiting and frustrating black and Latino voters.

What to do?

The only recourse was to take these states to court and demonstrate the discriminatory intent and effect of their electoral policies. This is exactly how Richard Nixon and his attorney general had hoped to gut the VRA in 1970. The long, litigious delays meant that, unlike the days of a robust and fully functioning Voting Rights Act, which prevented discrimination before it could do damage, the courts would now come in only after the fact.

Texas is a case in point. Almost the moment *Shelby County v. Holder* was announced, the Republican legislature put through a highly restrictive voter ID law, Senate Bill 14 (SB 14). A number of concerned citizens along with several organizations, including the NAACP and the League of United Latin American Citizens, immediately sued the state.

During the two-week trial in the fall of 2014, the attorney general of Texas, Greg Abbott, argued that the law was necessary to stop and prevent rampant voter-identification fraud.

Yet, out of ten million votes, Abbott could produce only *two* documented cases of voter impersonation. On the other hand, it became clear that nearly six hundred thousand Texans, mainly poor, black, and Latino, didn't have the newly required IDs and often faced financial and bureaucratic obstacles, which put these IDs out of reach for many.

In September 2014, in a stinging dressing-down of the state, district court judge Nelva Gonzales Ramos ruled that Texas's voter-ID law "creates an unconstitutional burden on the right to vote, has an impermissible discriminatory effect against Latinos and African Americans, and was imposed with an unconstitutional discriminatory purpose." Texas, she emphasized, had levied "an unconstitutional poll tax" on its citizens.

Ramos's ruling was a trip wire to reinstate the Voting Rights Act's Section 5 preclearance statute in Texas.

The state geared up to fight the decision. The first order of business, though, was to seek immediately a judicial delay to allow the voter ID law to remain in place during the upcoming midterm election.

Before the Fifth Circuit Court of Appeals, Texas attorney general Greg Abbott argued that chaos would reign at the polls if the voter ID law was changed so close to an election. Abbott also assured the court that keeping the voter ID law in place would not "substantially injure" the plaintiffs.

On October 14, 2014, the Fifth Circuit judges agreed. They granted Texas's request to allow a deliberately discriminatory law to operate during the all-important midterm election. As the judges saw it, "This is not a run-of-the-mill case" and Ramos's ruling "substantially disturbs the election process of the State of

Texas just nine days before early voting begins. Thus, the value of preserving the status quo here is much higher than in most other contexts."

The DOJ, civil rights groups, and individual voters then joined together and raced to the US Supreme Court, seeking to get it to overturn the Fifth Circuit's ruling. The US Supreme Court, led by Justice Antonin Scalia, ruled in favor of the state without any comment on the merits of SB 14.

Justice Ruth Bader Ginsburg's dissent was razor-sharp. It tore away at the supposed chaos that might occur in the election if the discredited voter-ID law was suddenly dropped. There "is little risk," wrote Ginsburg, of disrupting the election process. All Texas needed to do was "reinstate the voter identification procedure it employed for ten years (from 2003 to 2013) and in five federal general elections." After all, she observed, the new requirements for voter ID had only been used in three state elections where the voter turnout ranged from 1.48 percent to 9.98 percent. While those elections were relatively low-stakes, Ginsburg noted, the November 2014 election "would be the very first federal general election conducted" under the new voter-ID regime.

And that was the problem. The US Supreme Court, she wrote, could not allow a "purposefully discriminatory law, one that likely imposes an unconstitutional poll tax and risks denying the right to vote to hundreds of thousands of eligible voters" to be used in a federal election. But that is precisely what the US Supreme Court did.

After the election, the case went back to the Fifth Circuit Court of Appeals, as the US Department of Justice, civil rights groups, and a number of voters sought to invalidate SB 14 once and for all. In August 2015, the federal appeals court panel's deliberations focused on whether the legislature had actually intended to create a statute so blatantly discriminatory. The question of intent was central in determining whether Texas would have to undergo Section 5 preclearance scrutiny again. In a decision that fully satisfied neither of the parties, the panel of federal judges ruled that the Texas legislature had not set out to write a law that discriminated so clearly against Latinos and black Americans. However, the jurists continued, SB 14, the state's voter ID law, did violate what was left of the Voting Rights Act.

Confronted with being chastised for massive disenfranchisement, Greg Abbott, by then governor of Texas, continued the fiction that this law was about the sanctity of the ballot box. "Texas will continue to fight for its voter ID requirement to ensure the integrity of elections in the Lone Star State," he declared.

In addition to blocking access to the polls, the GOP disillusioned voters by making the very function of government so distasteful and haphazard that only the most diehard idealists or craven partisans would even bother to vote. Congressional Tea Party members bottled up legislation, confirmation hearings, and deliberations on pressing issues such as the economy—all to demonstrate how government does not and cannot function.

Casting Obama as uncompromising and irrational, in 2013 a Republican Congress shut down the federal government. This sixteen-day shutdown (October 1–October 17) cost the nation $24 billion. They then blamed the president.

These "public servants" seemed not to care what damage they did—even to their own reputations. Indeed, that was just the point: government—least of all under a black president—just does not function.

Public approval of Congress plummeted to the single digits. Indeed, one survey found that "Congress is less popular than hemorrhoids, jury duty and toenail fungus"—the result was that in the 2014 midterm elections, the United States had the lowest voter turnout since 1942. So many of those who had been mobilized and energized in 2008 were now disillusioned, demoralized, and, in many cases, disenfranchised.

Most simply stayed home on Election Day.

Mourners fill the room at a vigil at Emanuel African Methodist Episcopal Church in Charleston, South Carolina. In June 2015, nine black people were killed during a targeted shooting by a white man who attended a prayer service with the victims before turning a gun on them.

22

"WHY WOULD THEY TRY TO MAKE PEOPLE HATE US?"

THE VITRIOL HEAPED ON PRESIDENT OBAMA WAS simply unprecedented.

Barack Obama came to office with the nation perched on the edge of a financial abyss as foreclosures and the subprime mortgage crisis consumed $22 trillion in net wealth.

The nation's engagement in two endless, futile wars had led to thousands of American deaths (not to mention the hundreds of thousands of Iraqi and Afghani ones), and even more injuries, and these wars were running up a four- to six-trillion-dollar price tag.

Also, 16 percent of America's population lacked health insurance.

Obama's centrist solutions and utter lack of radicalism should have made him a hero to traditional Republicans. But just the opposite happened. By the end of his first term, the president had an 85.7 percent disapproval rating among the GOP.

The hatred started early. Before Obama was even a front-runner, the sheer number of racially motivated threats to his life prompted Secret Service protection. After he became the Democratic nominee, there was "a sharp and very disturbing increase in threats to Obama in September and early October [2008], at the same time that the crowds at [GOP vice presidential candidate Sarah] Palin rallies became more frenzied," reported *Newsweek*.

The heated, virulent rhetoric led Michelle Obama to ask, "Why would they try to make people hate us?"

In Obama's first year in office alone, there was a 400 percent increase in death threats, as compared to those received by one of the least popular presidents in American history, George W. Bush.

Facebook eventually shut down a page where hundreds answered yes to the question "Should Obama be killed?"

Nor was it just the "crazies." Supposedly respectable people tilled the hate-filled ground, lending an aura of authority to this campaign of terror. During the 2008 campaign, John McCain's strategists deliberately demonized not just Obama's policies but also the man himself. In the hatchet job they did on him, Obama mystically morphed into this Muslim, black nationalist, socialist, foreign, Arab, Kenyan, un-American immigrant monstrosity.

So vilified was Obama that the very office of the president ensured no respect. Breaking every rule of decorum and receiving millions of kudos for doing so, Republican South Carolina congressman Joe Wilson shouted at Obama, "You lie!" during a 2009 joint session of Congress.

Somehow many have convinced themselves that the man who pulled the United States back into some semblance of financial health, reduced unemployment to its lowest level in decades, secured health insurance for millions of citizens, ended one of our recent, all-too-intractable wars in the Middle East, reduced the staggering deficit he inherited from George W. Bush, and led the takedown of Osama bin Laden actually hated America.

In the run-up to the 2012 election, John Sununu, the former New Hampshire governor and an ally of Obama's presidential opponent, Mitt Romney, declared that he wished that "this president would learn to be an American."

In 2015, former New York mayor Rudy Giuliani told an audience, "I do not believe, and I know this is a horrible thing to say, but I do not believe that the president loves America. . . . He wasn't brought up the way you were brought up and I was brought up through the love of this country."

Many of those sworn to serve and protect couldn't contain their hatred of Obama. One New Hampshire police commissioner was observed sitting in a local diner glaring at the TV as he kept calling Obama a "f———g n———r." In North Canton, Ohio, a police dispatcher proudly sent out an e-mail to which she attached a manipulated image of Air Force One with the tail number NI66ER.

Then there's Ferguson, Missouri, where the second in command of the police force exchanged a series of e-mails with his lieutenant and a court official, depicting Barack Obama as a chimpanzee and doubting his ability as a black man to hold a job for four years.

Jelani Cobb wrote poignantly about the "paradox of progress" in his book *The Substance of Hope*. Sadly, the ascent of a black man to the presidency of the United States did not, despite all the talk of hope and a post-racial society, signal progress. Instead, not so unlike the days of Jim Crow, a sense of physical vulnerability was shared—and experienced—by men and women, and children across classes in the black community.

Sandra Bland, a woman driving to her new job at a Texas college, is pulled over for not using a turn signal, then jailed and later found dead in her cell.

A former college football player, Jonathan Ferrell, is injured in a car accident, seeks help, and is shot dead by the police.

A high school boy goes out of his house to purchase Skittles and iced tea, only to be stalked through the neighborhood by an armed man with a criminal record. Unarmed Trayvon Martin ends up dead. His shooter, George Zimmerman, is acquitted.

A twelve-year-old, Tamir Rice, is playing in the park with a toy gun. Police kill him within two seconds of their arrival.

A man merely makes eye contact with a police officer, and by the time Freddie Gray arrives at the jail, his neck is broken. He dies from this injury a week later.

A twenty-two-year-old woman is out with some friends when an off-duty police officer, thinking he sees something suspicious, fires into the crowd. The bullet slams into Rekia Boyd's skull, and she dies. The police officer is later acquitted.

Even when the wound is not fatal, it is grievous.

Endowed professor at Harvard Henry Louis Gates is arrested for being in his own house.

New York attorney and author Lawrence Otis Graham thought that teaching his children all the rules of respectability—dress, clothes, hair, behavior in public places—and showering them with all the education, vacations, and stable home life that money could afford would provide protection. He was wrong. His son's routine walk to class at a boarding school in New England became something much more as a carload of whites drove by and sliced through the child with the N-word as if it were a machete.

Just as in the past, black respectability or "appropriate" behavior doesn't seem to matter. If anything, black achievement, black aspirations, and black success are construed as direct threats. Obama's presidency made that clear. Aspirations and the achievement of these aspirations provide no protection. Not even to the God-fearing.

On June 17, 2015, South Carolinian Dylann Storm Roof, a white, unemployed twenty-one-year-old high school dropout, was on a mission to "take his country back."

Ever since George Zimmerman walked out of the courthouse a free man after killing Trayvon Martin, and a racially polarized nation debated the verdict, Roof had looked to understand the history of America. Trolling through the internet, he stumbled across the Council of Conservative Citizens (CCC), offspring of the 1950s White Citizens' Council, which had terrorized black people, closed schools, and worked hand in hand with state governments to defy federal civil rights laws. The CCC's intentions on the web were cleverly masked, skewing the facts, rewriting history, and draped in the flag to lend an aura of authority and respectability.

The CCC's core values center on a Christianity that justifies slavery, embraces racially homogenous societies, and emphasizes blacks as a "retrograde species of humanity." But despite the group's avowed racist belief system, in the mid to late 1990s, it "boasted of having 34 members who were in the Mississippi legislature and had powerful Republican Party allies, including then–Senate Majority Leader Trent Lott of Mississippi," reported the Southern Poverty Law Center.

By 2004, Mississippi governor Haley Barbour, the chair of the Republican National Committee, and thirty-seven other powerful politicians had all attended CCC events in the twenty-first century. In 2013, it was discovered that Roan Garcia-Quintana, a Tea Party stalwart on South Carolina governor Nikki Haley's reelection steering committee, was a CCC board member. What's more, the Council of Conservative Citizens' chair, Earl Holt III, gave "$65,000 to Republican campaign funds in recent years," reported the *Guardian* in 2015. That money included donations to the 2016 presidential campaigns of Rand Paul, Republican from Kentucky; Rick Santorum, Republican from Pennsylvania; and Ted Cruz, Republican from Texas.

The CCC, then, enjoyed precisely the cachet of respectability that racism requires to achieve its own goals within American society. And its website of hatred and lies provided the self-serving education Dylann Roof so desperately craved. He drank in the poison of its message, got into his car, drove to Charleston, entered Emanuel AME Church, and landed in a Bible study with a group of black Americans who were the very model of respectability. Roof prayed with them. Read the Bible with them. Thought they were "so nice." Then he shot them dead, leaving just one woman alive so that she could tell the world what he had done and why.

"You're taking over our country," he said.

EPILOGUE

IMAGINE.

In July 2015, not even a full month after Dylann Roof gunned down nine black people at Emanuel AME Church in Charleston, South Carolina, Republican front-runner Donald Trump fired up his "silent majority" audience of thousands with a macabre promise: "Don't worry, we'll take our country back."

It is time instead that we the people take our country forward.

More than a century and a half of anger and fear have undermined American democracy, trampled the constitution, and treated some citizens as chattel and others as collateral damage.

This did not have to be. The Land of Opportunity did not have to be the Land of Missed Opportunities.

It is time to defuse the power of white rage.

It is time to move into a future where the right to vote is unfettered by discriminatory restrictions that prevent millions of American citizens from having any say in their own government.

It is time to move into a future that invests in our children by making access to good schools the norm, not the exception, and certainly not dependent upon zip code. We know the consequences of dysfunctional school systems. We see the wasted lives, just as clearly as Eisenhower and Congressman Carl Elliott saw them during the Sputnik crisis.

We can choose not to listen to the rage and, instead, craft a stronger, more viable future for this nation. We can ask tough questions such as: Why use property taxes as the basis for funding schools when that method rewards discriminatory public policy and perpetuates the inequalities that undermine our society?

The future is one that takes seriously a justice system whose enormous powers are actually used to serve and protect. The misuse is storied—from the convict-lease labor system to one that is now employed to undercut the gains of the Civil Rights Movement. A program that stops and frisks mostly those who are the least likely to have illegal contraband is not law enforcement.

It is time to rethink America.

Imagine if Reconstruction had actually honored the citizenship of four million freed people—provided the education, political autonomy, and economic wherewithal warranted by their and their ancestors' hundreds of years of free labor.

Imagine if, instead of continually refighting the Civil War, we had actually moved on to rebuilding a strong, viable South, a South where poor whites, too—for they had been left out as well—could gain access to proper education.

Imagine the educational prowess our population might now

boast had *Brown* actually been implemented. What a very different nation we would be if all the enormous legal and political efforts that went into subverting and undermining the right to education had actually been used to uphold and ensure that right. If all those hundreds upon hundreds of millions of federal dollars poured into science education had actually rained down on those hungry for education, regardless of race, ethnicity, or income. Think about what a different national conversation we might be having, even as the economy turns ever more surely to knowledge-based industries, rather than watching our share of the world's scientists and engineers dwindle.

Imagine if the Civil Rights Movement had really resulted in Martin Luther King's Beloved Community.

What if all the billions of dollars that have been diverted into militarizing police for a phony war on drugs and building prison after prison had been devoted instead to education, to housing, to health care?

Imagine if, instead of launching into spurious attacks about President Obama's citizenship and filling the blogosphere with racist simian depictions, the United States had been able to harness the awe-inspiring symbolism of our first black president.

We shouldn't have to imagine.

Full voting rights for American citizens, funding and additional resources for quality schools, and policing and court systems in which racial bias is not sanctioned by law—all these are well within our grasp. Visionaries, activists, judges, and politicians before us saw what America could be and fought hard for that kind of nation.

This is the moment now when all of us—black, white,

Latino, Native American, Asian American—must step out of the shadow of white rage, deny its power, understand its unseemly goals, and refuse to be seduced by its buzzwords, dog whistles, and sophistry.

This is when we choose a different future.

DISCUSSION GUIDE

1. *We Are Not Yet Equal* introduces the concept of "white rage." How does this concept differ from the other ways you may have thought about race relations in the past? What assumptions about race relations did you have coming into this book? Does the book contradict or support these assumptions?

2. This book focuses on certain watershed periods of US history, from the Civil War to President Obama's second term. Why do you think the author chose to examine these times specifically? Are there other moments in history that can be looked at through the scope of white rage?

3. For some, legality and morality might intersect, but there are many instances in this book where the author shows lawmakers, judges, and politicians using the law to serve their white rage. What are some instances from the book in which these occur? Can you think of other examples from current events where this has happened, too?

4. What are ways in which people today can respond to white rage? How can individuals respond to legal and government systems that indicate biases? What changes do legal and government systems need to make?

5. What role has the media played in perpetuating violence and inequity against black Americans? Has this changed over time? What are some ways that you can identify media biases?

6. In what ways has American history influenced everyday life for black people today? In which systems do we still see the roots of slavery?

7. How and where are teens affected by white rage? Do teens experience its effects differently than adults? Why or why not? How do these dynamics play out in a school setting?

8. Is it possible to discuss racial politics without considering class and gender issues? How do they intersect in this book? How do you see them intersect in the world today?

9. This book focuses primarily on black Americans and black history. How do the author's arguments affect how you view the broader scope of US history?

10. Think about the title of this book. Do you agree with its assertion? What does the word "yet" imply? How do you see the future of racial equality in the United States?

FOR FURTHER READING

Buried in the Bitter Waters: The Hidden History of Racial Cleansing in America by Elliot Jaspin (Basic Books, 2007).

Freedom Summer Murders by Don Mitchell (Scholastic, 2014).

From the War on Poverty to the War on Crime: The Making of Mass Incarceration in America by Elizabeth Hinton (Harvard University Press, 2016).

The March Trilogy by John Lewis, Andrew Aydin, and Nate Powell (Top Shelf, 2013, 2015, 2016).

The New Jim Crow: Mass Incarceration in the Age of Colorblindness by Michelle Alexander (The New Press, 2010).

Stamped from the Beginning: The Definitive History of Racist Ideas in America by Ibram X. Kendi (Nation Books, 2016).

We Were Eight Years in Power: An American Tragedy by Ta-Nehisi Coates (One World, 2017).

A Wreath for Emmett Till by Marilyn Nelson (Houghton Mifflin Harcourt, 2005).

NOTES

PROLOGUE

xiv "community's racism against the police": *Nightline*, "America in Black and White: The Shooting of Amadou Diallo," ABC, February 26, 1999.

1 "ORIGINAL SIN"

p. 1 "original sin": Alexander Tsesis, ed., *The Promises of Liberty: The History and Contemporary Relevance of the Thirteenth Amendment* (New York: Columbia University Press, 2010), xviii.

p. 1 "Indeed I tremble": "Personal Freedom," PBS, http://www.pbs.org /jefferson/enlight/person.htm.

p. 2 on Civil War casualties: James M. McPherson, "In Pursuit of Constitutional Abolitionism," in *The Promises of Liberty*, ed. Tsesis, 27; "Civil War Casualties. The Cost of War: Killed, Captured, Wounded, and Missing," http://www.civilwar.org/education/civil-war-casualties.html, accessed January 25, 2015.

p. 2 "all the wealth": "Second Inaugural Address of Abraham Lincoln," Saturday, March 4, 1865, http://avalon.law.yale.edu/19th_century/lincoln2 .asp, accessed November 6, 2015.

2 "BUT FOR YOUR RACE"

p. 7 "But for your race": "Lincoln's Panama Plan," *New York Times*, August 16, 2012, http://opinionator.blogs.nytimes.com/2012/08/16/lincolns -panama-plan/?r=0, accessed November 22, 2015.

p. 7 "We will work": "Black Residents of Nashville to the Union Convention," January 9, 1865, http://www.freedmen.umd.edu/tenncon.htm, accessed February 25, 2015.

p. 7 "What did we go to war for": A. J. Langguth, *After Lincoln: How the North Won the Civil War and Lost the Peace* (New York: Simon and Schuster, 2014), 61.

p. 7 "Our position is throughly": "A Declaration of the Immediate Causes Which Induce and Justify the Secession of the State of Mississippi from the Federal Union," Avalon Project, Lillian Goldman Law Library, Yale Law School, http://avalon.law.yale.edu/19th_century/csa_missec.asp, accessed January 27, 2015.

p. 7 on South Carolina's wealth: "The Condition of Affairs in South Carolina," *Liberator*, June 23, 1865, 1.

p. 8 on wealthiest Americans: David Brian Davis, "The Rocky Road to Freedom," in *The Promises of Liberty*, ed. Tsesis, xvii.

p. 9 "Black men and black women were attacked . . . men, women, and children watched": Leslie M. Harris, "The New York City Draft Riots of 1863," excerpt from *In the Shadow of Slavery: African Americans in New York City, 1626–1863*, http://www.press.uchicago.edu/Misc/Chicago/317749 .html, accessed February 19, 2015.

p. 11 Thirteenth Amendment: "Transcript of 13th Amendment to the US Constitution: Abolition of Slavery (1865)," Our Documents, https://www .ourdocuments.gov/doc.php?flash=false&doc=40&page=transcript, accessed April 9, 2018.

p. 11 "What is Freedom? . . . a cruel delusion": Burke A. Hindale, ed. *The Works of James Abram Garfield*, vol. 1 (Boston: James R. Osgood and Company, 1882), 86.

p. 11 "We claim freedom": "Black Residents of Nashville to the Union Convention," January 9, 1865, http://www.freedmen.umd.edu/tenncon.htm, accessed February 25, 2015.

3 FORTY ACRES AND A MULE

p. 16 "Howard was . . . thankless duty": W. E. B. Du Bois, *Black Reconstruction in America: 1865–1880* (New York: Touchstone, 1995), 223.

p. 18 "traitors": Annette Gordon-Reed, *Andrew Johnson* (New York: Times Books, 2011), 113.

p. 18 "must be punished and impoverished": Michael A. Ross, *Justice of Shattered Dreams: Samuel Freeman Miller and the Supreme Court during the Civil War Era* (Baton Rouge: Louisiana State University Press, 2003), 105–6.

p. 18 "Freedom is not . . . character": Langguth, *After Lincoln*, 134.

p. 19 Andrew Johnson's first proclamation: "Proclamation 134—Granting Amnesty to Participants in the Rebellion, with Certain Exceptions," The American Presidency Project, http://www.presidency.ucsb .edu/ws/index.php?pid=72392.

p. 19 Andrew Johnson's second proclamation: "Proclamation 135—Reorganizing a Constitutional Government in North Carolina," The American Presidency Project, http://www.presidency.ucsb.edu/ws/index.php ?pid=72403.

p. 20 Carl Schurz's findings: "Report on the Condition of the South by Carl Schurz," first published 1865, 39th Congress, Senate, 1st Session, Ex. Doc. No. 2, 89–91, http://www.wwnorton.com/college/history/give-me -liberty4/docs/.

p. 20 "staggering proportions": Gordon-Reed, *Andrew Johnson*, 117.

p. 20 "Not only . . . under these conditions": Gordon-Reed, *Andrew Johnson*, 118.

p. 21 "We hold this to be . . . citizens of the United States": Louisiana Democratic Platform, October 2, 1865, in Walter F. Fleming, ed., *Documentary History of Reconstruction*, vol. 1 (Cleveland, OH: The Arthur H. Clark Company, 1906), 229.

p. 21 "no rights which the white man": *Dred Scott v. Sandford*, 60 US 393 (1857), http://www.oxfordreference.com/view/10.1093/acref/9780195088786 .001.0001/acref-9780195088786-e-0268.

p. 21 "a country for white men . . . government for white men": Gordon-Reed, *Andrew Johnson*, 112.

p. 21 "held up before us": Gordon-Reed, *Andrew Johnson*, 118–19.

p. 21 "right and power . . .": Eric Foner, *Reconstruction: America's Unfinished Revolution, 1863–1877* (New York: Harper and Row, 1988), 199.

4 BLACK CODES

p. 23 "were an astonishing . . . but name": Du Bois, *Black Reconstruction*, 167.

p. 24 on Mississippi's Black Codes: *Laws of the State of Mississippi, Passed at a Regular Session of the Mississippi Legislature, Held in Jackson, October, November, and December, 1865* (Jackson, 1866), 82–93, 165–67; Leon F. Litwack, *Been in the Storm So Long: The Aftermath of Slavery* (New York: Random House, 1980), 368; David M. Oshinsky, *"Worse Than Slavery": Parchman Farm and the Ordeal of Jim Crow Justice* (New York: Free Press, 1996), 21.

p. 24 "a form of vagrancy . . . ," "the first ten days . . . ," and "orphans were sent . . .": Langguth, *After Lincoln*, 109.

p. 24 "If you call this Freedom": Foner, *Reconstruction*, 215.

p. 25 "encouraging unrealistic expectations": Langguth, *After Lincoln*, 108–9.

p. 25 articles in the *North American and United States Gazette*: "Labor in the Rebel States" and "What the South Has Done," November 18, 1865.

p. 26 "too much the poor man's friend": St. George L. Sioussat, "Andrew Johnson and the Early Phases of the Homestead Bill," *Mississippi Valley Historical Association* 5, no. 3 (December 1918), 276.

5 "WE SHOWED OUR HAND TOO SOON"

p. 32 "We showed our hand . . . everything our own way": Litwack, *Been in the Storm So Long*, 368.

p. 33 on the failure of the Freedmen's Bureau Bill: "Veto of the Freedmen's Bureau Bill," February 19, 1866, http://teachingamericanhistory.org/library/document/veto-of-the-freedmens-bureau-bill, accessed February 24, 2015.

p. 35 "After the boy spent . . .": Langguth, *After Lincoln*, 55.

p. 35–36 "all northern men . . . ignore work": "Labor in the Rebel States," *North American and United States Gazette*, November 18, 1865.

p. 36 "The idea that he": Langguth, *After Lincoln*, 110.

p. 36–37 "racist, biased, obstructionist . . . unpunished violence": Michael A. Ross, *Justice of Shattered Dreams*, 114.

p. 37 "The planters believed": James D. Anderson, *The Education of Blacks in the South, 1860–1935* (Chapel Hill: University of North Carolina Press, 1988), 4.

p. 38 "a slave by the name": Anderson, *The Education of Blacks in the South*, 17.

p. 38 Thomas Conway's report: Langguth, *After Lincoln*, 113–14.

p. 38 "an effort is being made . . . 500 schools": Anderson, *The Education of Blacks in the South*, 6–7.

p. 38 "with a fundamentally . . . oppression": Anderson, *The Education of Blacks in the South*, 17.

p. 39 On Johnson's veto of the Civil Rights Act: March 27, 1866, http://teachingamericanhistory.org/library/document/veto-of-the-civil-rights-bill, accessed February 24, 2015.

6 "JOHNSON IS WITH US!"

p. 41 "Johnson is with us!" Langguth, *After Lincoln*, 148.

p. 44 Fourteenth Amendment: "Transcript of 14th Amendment to the US Constitution: Civil Rights (1868)," Our Documents, https://www.ourdocuments.gov/doc.php?flash=false&doc=43&page=transcript.

p. 46 Fifteenth Amendment: "Transcript of 15th Amendment to the US Constitution: Voting Rights (1870)," Our Documents, https://www.ourdocuments.gov/doc.php?flash=false&doc=44&page=transcript.

7 COURTING JUSTICE

p. 49 "in most of the Southern States": Frederick Douglass, *Life and Times of Frederick Douglass* (De Wolfe & Fiske Co.: Boston, 1892), 611.

p. 51 "citizens still had to seek": Ross, *Justice of Shattered Dreams*, 200.

p. 52 "had merely prevented": Bruce R. Trimble, *Chief Justice Waite: Defender of the Public Interest* (Princeton, NJ: Princeton University Press, 1938), 162; United States v. Reese et al., 92 US 214 (1876).

p. 52 on Colfax massacre: Foner, *Reconstruction*, 437.

p. 52 on *United States v. Cruikshank*: Trimble, *Chief Justice Waite*, 168; *Cruikshank*, 92 US 542 (1876).

p. 54 on the Civil Rights cases: "The Civil Rights Cases, 109 US 3 (1883)," Justia, https://supreme.justia.com/cases/federal/us/109/3/case.html.

p. 54 "crypto-slavery . . . of the laws": William Wiecek, "Emancipation and Civic Status," in *The Promises of Liberty*, ed. Tsesis, 90, 95, 93.

p. 55 "If one race be inferior . . . that construction upon it": *"Plessy v. Ferguson* 163 US 537 (1896)," https://supreme.justia.com/cases/federal/us /163/537/case.html.

p. 56 on the poll tax: Manfred Berg, *"The Ticket to Freedom": The NAACP and the Struggle for Black Political Integration* (Gainesville: University of Florida Press, 2005), 105.

p. 56–57 "Why apologize . . . equal of a white man": Wiecek, "Emancipation and Civic Status," in *The Promises of Liberty,* ed. Tsesis, 90.

p. 57 the federal courts: Wiecek, "Emancipation and Civic Status," in *The Promises of Liberty,* ed. Tsesis, 94.

8 DERAILING THE GREAT MIGRATION

p. 59 "safe for democracy": "Making the World 'Safe for Democracy': Woodrow Wilson Asks for War," http://historymatters.gmu.edu/d/4943, accessed November 7, 2015.

p. 60 "five days lynching orgy": "11 Lynched Instead of 6 as First Reported in Georgia: Names of Ringleaders Known," *Philadelphia Tribune,* September 7, 1918, 8.

p. 61 "riddled with bullets": "Memorandum for Governor Dorsey from Walter F. White", July 10, 1918, http://www.maryturner.org/images /memorandum.pdf, accessed October 25, 2015.

p. 62 on lynching and the rape of black women in the South: Dray, *At the Hands of Persons Unknown;* "Lynchings by State and Race: 1882–1968," http:// law2.umkc.edu/faculty/projects/ftrials/shipp/lynchingsstate.html, accessed November 8, 2015; Amy Louise Wood, *Lynching and Spectacle: Witnessing Racial Violence in America, 1890–1940* (Chapel Hill: University of North Carolina Press, 2011); William H. Chafe, Raymond Gavins, and Robert Korstad, ed., *Remembering Jim Crow: African Americans Tell About Life in the Segregated South* (New York: New Press, 2001), 206–7, 211–16; Danielle McGuire, *At the Dark End of the Street: Black Women, Rape and Resistance—a New History of the Civil Rights Movement from Rosa Parks to the Rise of Black Power* (New York: Knopf, 2010).

p. 62 on the exodus from south Georgia: "Memorandum for Governor Dorsey from Walter F. White." July 10, 1918, http://www.maryturner.org /images/memorandum.pdf, accessed October 25, 2015.

p. 62 "willing to run . . . breathe freer": James R. Grossman, *Land of Hope: Chicago, Black Southerners, and the Great Migration* (Chicago: University of Chicago, 1991), 16.

p. 62 on European immigration: Ethan Michaeli, *The Defender: How the Legendary Black Newspaper Changed America: From the Age of the Pullman Porters to the Age of Obama* (New York: Houghton Mifflin Harcourt, 2016), 63.

p. 63 "Hell": Grossman, *Land of Hope*, 60.

p. 63 "Whenever the colored man . . . britches off you": Grossman, *Land of Hope*, 34.

p. 63 "Better not accumulate much . . . can't enjoy it": Grossman, *Land of Hope*, 34.

p. 63 "whitecapping" and "ride for miles": Grossman, *Land of Hope*, 17.

p. 63 on sharecropping: Isabel Wilkerson, *The Warmth of Other Suns: The Epic Story of America's Great Migration* (New York: Vintage Books, 2011), 166, 167, 170; *Oh Freedom After While*, directed by Steven John Ross and narrated by Julian Bond (California Newsreel, 1999), 56 minutes, DVD.

p. 64 on education in a Mississippi county and in Dawson County, Georgia: "Sharecropper Migration," *American Experience*, PBS, http://www.pbs.org/wgbh/americanexperience/features/generalarticle/flood-sharecroppers, accessed June 21, 2015; Leon F. Litwack, *Trouble in Mind: Black Southerners in the Age of Jim Crow* (New York: Vintage Books, 1998), 37.

p. 66 "Vigorous protests . . . so great as to call for action": "Luring Labor North," *Times-Picayune*, August 22, 1916, 4.

p. 66 On labor agent license in Macon: Roi Ottley, *The Lonely Warrior: The Life and Times of Robert S. Abbott* (Chicago: H. Regnery Co., 1955), 165.

p. 67 On labor agent license in Jacksonville: Emmett J. Scott, *Negro Migration During the War*, Carnegie Endowment for International Peace: Preliminary Economic Studies of the War, no. 16, ed. David Kinley (New York: Oxford University Press, 1920), 37.

p. 67 "and a rope and a gun in . . . the toe of my shoe": Spencer R. Crew, *Field to Factory: Afro-American Migration, 1915–1940* (Washington, DC: National Museum of American History, 1987), 6–7.

p. 68 "Get out of the South": Ottley, *The Lonely Warrior*, p. 163.

p. 68 "You see they are not lifting . . . white women": Ottley, *The Lonely Warrior*, 165–66.

p. 71 "We are not slaveholders . . . we cannot compel them to stay here": "Letters to the Telegraph," *Macon Daily Telegraph*, August 28, 1916, 4.

p. 71 1.5 million: "The Second Great Migration," http://www.inmotionaame.org/print.cfm?migration=9, accessed June 4, 2018.

9 THE SWEET ORDEAL

p. 73 **"More Thousands Kiss the South a Last Good-By":** *Chicago Defender*, December 30, 1922, 4.

p. 74 **on Ford:** Steven Watts, *The People's Tycoon: Henry Ford and the American Century* (New York: Knopf, 2005), 178–87.

p. 74 **on Detroit's black population growth:** Scott Martelle, *Detroit: A Biography* (Chicago: Chicago Review Press, 2012), 85; Kevin Boyle, *Arc of Justice: A Saga of Race, Civil Rights, and Murder in the Jazz Age* (New York: Owl Books, 2004), 7.

p. 75 **on housing for black Detroit:** Boyle, *Arc of Justice*, 9; Walter White, *A Man Called White: The Autobiography of Walter White* (New York: Viking Press, 1948; Athens, GA: a Brown Thraser Book, University of Georgia, 1995), 73; Martelle, *Detroit*, 90–91.

p. 77 **"It looked like a human sea . . . faster":** John A. Farrell, *Clarence Darrow: Attorney for the Damned* (New York: Vintage Books, 2012), 413.

p. 78 **"caught snatches of bitterness . . .":** Boyle, *Arc of Justice*, 19.

p. 79 **"near death from . . . fatal":** "Put Guard on Home of Negro," *Detroit Times*, September 10, 1925, 1.

p. 79 **Mayor Smith's open letter:** Boyle, *Arc of Justice*, 195–96.

p. 81 **Exchange between Kennedy and Schuknecht:** Boyle, *Arc of Justice*, 187.

p. 82 **"the Sweets would face an all-white jury . . . didn't deserve his salary":** Boyle, *Arc of Justice*, 186.

p. 82 **Exchange between Kennedy and Dr. Sweet:** Boyle, *Arc of Justice*, 174.

p. 83 **"began coming in one me":** Boyle, *Arc of Justice*, 178.

p. 83 **"shot through the back . . . cold-blooded murder":** Farrell, *Clarence Darrow*, 417.

p. 83–84 **"The importance . . . throughout the country":** White, *A Man Called White*, 74–75.

p. 84–85 **"perjured themselves . . . original sin":** Farrell, *Clarence Darrow*, 413, 415.

p. 85 **"many of the prosecution witnesses . . .":** James Weldon Johnson, "Detroit Mob Violence Case," in Sondra Kathryn Wilson, *In Search* *of Democracy: The NAACP and the Writings of James Weldon Johnson, Walter White and Roy Wilkins, 1920–1977* (New York: Oxford University Press, 1999), 74.

p. 85 "There is nothing but prejudice . . .": Farrell, *Clarence Darrow*, 423.

10 BUILDING TOWARD *BROWN*

p. 91 on education and income in Delaware: Peter Irons, *Jim Crow's Children: The Broken Promise of the Brown Decision* (New York: Penguin Books, 2002), 108–9.

p. 92 "was jammed with more than": Irons, *Jim Crow's Children*, 82.

p. 92 "Chicken coops": "A View from Virginia," *Washington Post*, May 13, 2004, C14, http://www.washingtonpost.com/wp-dyn/articles/A22021 -2004May12.html.

p. 92 "to show people": Jill Ogline Titus, *Brown's Battleground: Students, Segregationists and the Struggle for Justice in Prince Edward County, Virginia* (Chapel Hill: University of North Carolina Press, 2011), 3.

p. 92 black schools in Prince Edward County: Titus, *Brown's Battleground*, 4.

p. 93 "overcrowded classrooms . . . during the 1947–48 school year": Tomiko Brown-Nagin, *Courage to Dissent: Atlanta and the Long History of the Civil Rights Movement* (New York: Oxford University Press, 2011), 95–96, 445.

p. 93 on black education in Louisiana: State Department of Education of Louisiana, "Ninety-Fifth Annual Report for the Session 1943–44," Bulletin No. 543 (December 1944), 170–71.

p. 94 on formal education in Alabama, Georgia, Louisiana, South Carolina, and Mississippi: Jessie Parkhurst Guzman, ed., *Negro Year Book: A Review of Events Affecting Negro Life, 1941–1946* (Tuskegee, AL: Tuskegee Institute, 1947), 70; US Department of Commerce, Bureau of the Census, 1950 United States Census of Population, Series PC-14 (Washington, DC: Government Printing Office, 1953), 4.

p. 96 "scramble": Roy Wilkins, *Standing Fast: The Autobiography of Roy Wilkins* (New York: Da Capo Press, 1994), 218.

p. 96 "I offered my life": Irons, *Jim Crow's Children*, 87.

p. 97 "Before it was over . . . consume the night": Richard Kluger, *Simple Justice: The History of Brown v. Board of Education and Black America's Struggle for Equality* (New York: Vintage Books, 2004), 3.

p. 97 "We will protect": Wilkins, *Standing Fast*, 233–34.

p. 97 "regardless of consequences": Numan V. Bartley, *The Rise of Massive Resistance: Race and Politics in the South During the 1950s* (Baton Rouge: Louisiana State University Press, 1999), 46.

p. 97 "as long as . . . Negroes will not be admitted to white schools": Bartley, *The Rise of Massive Resistance*, 41.

p. 98 on the more than three hundred thousand black children in Georgia in 1950: US Department of Commerce, Bureau of the Census, Census Population: 1950, pt. 11, vol. 2, by Howard G. Brunsman (Washington, DC: Government Printing Office, 1952), 214.

p. 98 "Of only one thing . . . in our schools": Bartley, *The Rise of Massive Resistance*, 46.

p. 99 "are not bad people": Stephen E. Ambrose, *Eisenhower: The President*, vol. 2 (New York: Simon and Schuster, 1984), 190.

p. 99 cost of equalizing schools: Carol Anderson, *Eyes Off the Prize: The United Nations and the African American Struggle for Human Rights, 1944–1955* (Boston, Cambridge University Press, 2003), 12.

p. 99 "If segregation is unconstitutional": Angie Maxwell, *The Indicted South: Public Criticism, Southern Inferiority, and the Politics of Whiteness* (Chapel Hill: University of North Carolina Press, 2014), 194.

p. 99 "the most exciting moment . . . that follow them": Maxwell, *The Indicted South,*193.

p. 100 *Brown* opinion: "Transcript of *Brown v. Board of Education* (1954)," Our Documents, https://www.ourdocuments.gov/doc.php?flash=false&doc=87&page=transcript.

p. 101 "the greatest victory": John Kyle Day, *The Southern Manifesto: Massive Resistance and the Fight to Preserve Segregation* (Jackson: University of Mississippi Press, 2014), 7.

p. 101 "May 17, 1954": Wilkins, *Standing Fast*, 214.

p. 101 "my sense of euphoria": Wilkins, *Standing Fast*, 215.

11 BEATING DOWN *BROWN*

p. 105 "with all deliberate speed": *Brown v. Board of Education*, 349 US 294 (1955), Justia, https://supreme.justia.com/cases/federal/us/349/294/case.html.

p. 105 "serve notice on": Bartley, *The Rise of Massive Resistance*, 127.

p. 105–06 "condemns and protests against . . . United States": Day, *The Southern Manifesto*, 14.

p. 106 "We do not advocate . . . within the law": Day, *The Southern Manifesto*, 10.

p. 107 on the Southern Manifesto: "The Southern Manifesto of 1956," March 12, 1956, US House of Representatives History, Art, and Archives, http://history.house.gov/Historical-Highlights/1951-2000/The-Southern -Manifesto-of-1956, accessed June 28, 2015.

p. 107 "If we can organize . . . in the South": "Brown at 60: The Southern Manifesto and 'Massive Resistance' to Brown, NAACP Legal Defense and Education Fund, http://www.naacpldf.org/brown-at-60 -southern-manifesto-and-massive-resistance-brown.

p. 108 "As long as we can legislate": Charles J. Ogletree Jr., *All Deliberate Speed: Reflections on the First Half-Century of Brown v. Board of Education* (New York: W. W. Norton, 2004), 130–31.

p. 108 "the Court's interpretation": Ogletree, *All Deliberate Speed*, 129–30.

p. 109 "black children in Little Rock . . .": Wilkins, *Standing Fast*, 258.

p. 109 on the thirteen thousand white students: "James Lindsay Almond," *Dictionary of Virginia*, http://www.lva.virginia.gov/public/dvb/bio .asp?b=Almond_James_Lindsay, accessed June 4, 2018.

p. 109 "Pundits wasted no time": Titus, *Brown's Battleground*, 19.

p. 110 "little more than a scant": "The Forgotten Children of the 'New Frontier': Prince Edward County," *Afro-American*, April 8, 1961.

p. 111 "denied that the Virginia constitution": "Prince Edward Says Schools Not Required," *Washington Post*, July 7, 1961.

p. 111 "employed every weapon": Titus, *Brown's Battleground*, 10.

p. 111 "an interrupted education": Bob Smith, *They Closed Their Schools: Prince Edward County, Virginia, 1951–64* (Chapel Hill: University of North Carolina Press, 1965), 147.

p. 111–12 on John Hurt's story: Christopher Bonastia, *Southern Stalemate: Five Years without Public Education in Prince Edward County, Virginia* (Chicago: University of Chicago Press, 2012), 157.

p. 112 "rather his children . . . attack or criticize": Liza Mundy, "Making Up for Lost Time: Virginia Has Created a Scholarship Program to Give African American Adults from Prince Edward County Something They

Were Denied as Children: An Education," *Washington Post*, November 5, 2006.

p. 113 **"black parents"**: Bonastia, *Southern Stalemate*, 7.

p. 113 **"painted the federal courts"**: Titus, *Brown's Battleground*, 32–33.

12 THE NAACP AND SPUTNIK

p. 115 **"There was nothing abstract"**: Wilkins, *Standing Fast*, 222.

p. 117–18 **on Eastland and Gathings:** Bartley, *The Rise of Massive Resistance*, 186, 120, 186.

p. 118 **"proof of the fact"**: Robert Divine, *The Sputnik Challenge: Eisenhower's Response to the Soviet Satellite* (New York: Oxford University Press, 1993), xiv–xv.

p. 118 **"shaken by . . . rocketry"**: John Finney, "US Missile Experts Shaken by Sputnik: Weight of Satellite Seen as Evidence of Soviet Superiority in Rocketry," *New York Times*, October 13, 1957.

p. 119 **"This is confirmation . . . irresistible"**: "The Military Meaning," *Washington Post*, October 8, 1957.

p. 119–20 **"a second-class power" and "Two Sputniks cannot sway Eisenhower"**: Matthew Brzenzinski, *Red Moon Rising: Sputnik and the Hidden Rivalries That Ignited the Space Age* (New York: Times Books, 2007), 221.

p. 120 **"the loss of a student"**: Barbara Barksdale Clowse, *Brainpower for the Cold War: The Sputnik Crisis and National Defense Education Act of 1958* (Westport, CT: Greenwood Press, 1981), 102.

p. 120 **"equipped to live in the age"**: Divine, *The Sputnik Challenge*, 55.

p. 121 **"in the context . . . happen to America"**: Clowse, *Brainpower for the Cold War*, 37–38, 50, 52–53, 102.

p. 121 **"gap between what the Negro"**: Day, *The Southern Manifesto*, 6.

p. 121 **"mobilize [its] brainpower"**: Clowse, *Brainpower for the Cold War*, 4.

p. 122 **"no single event . . . to survive and prosper"**: Dwight D. Eisenhower to Swede Hazlett, July 27, 1957, http://www.eisenhower.archives.gov/research/online_documents/civil_rights_brown_v_boe/1957_07_22_DDE_to_Hazlett.pdf, accessed November 14, 2015.

p. 123 **"threatening to withold"**: Clowse, *Brainpower for the Cold War*, 43.

p. 123 "He stated that integration": Clowse, *Brainpower for the Cold War*, 121.

p. 124 on black PhDs in STEM: "Doctoral Degree Awards to African Americans Reach Another All-Time High," *Journal of Blacks in Higher Education*, 2006, http://www.jbhe.com/news_views/50_black _doctoraldegrees.html, accessed July 11, 2015. (Note that the growth cited in this article is driven overwhelmingly by doctorates in education.)

p. 124 Adkins's data: Rodney C. Adkins, "America Desperately Needs More STEM Students. Here's How to Get Them," *Forbes* July 9, 2012, http:// www.forbes.com/sites/forbesleadershipforum/2012/07/09/america -desperately-needs-more-stem-students-heres-how-to-get-them, accessed July 11, 2015.

p. 125 "satisfy the federal courts . . . community": Sondra Gordy, *Finding the Lost Year: What Happened When Little Rock Closed Its Public Schools* (Fayetteville, AR: University of Arkansas Press, 2009), 170, 171.

13 ROLLING BACK CIVIL RIGHTS

p. 130 "to redeem the soul of America": Adam Fairclough, *To Redeem the Soul of America: The Southern Christian Leadership Conference and Martin Luther King, Jr.* (Athens, GA: University of Georgia Press, 2001), 32.

p. 131 "This law covers . . . struck down": "Remarks in the Capitol Rotunda at the Signing of the Voting Rights Act," The American Presidency Project, http://www.presidency.ucsb.edu/ws/?pid=27140.

p. 132 Civil Rights Act of 1964: "Transcript of Civil Rights Act (1964)," Our Documents, https://www.ourdocuments.gov/doc.php ?flash=false&doc=97&page=transcript.

p. 134 "America has been the best country" Patrick J. Buchanan, "A Brief for Whitey," March 21, 2008, http://buchanan.org/blog/pjb-a-brief-for -whitey-969, accessed July 31, 2015.

p. 134 Voting Rights Act of 1965: "Voting Rights Act (1965)," Our Documents, https://www.ourdocuments.gov/doc.php?flash=false&doc=100& page=transcript.

p. 135 "government handout . . . rather than work": Stephanie Greco Larson, *Media and Minorities: The Politics of Race in News and Entertainment* (Lanham, MD: Rowman and Littlefield, 2006), 90–91.

p. 136 "Will you join in . . . mind and spirit": "Lyndon B. Johnson: Remarks at the University of Michigan, May 22, 1964," The American Presidency Project, http://www.presidency.ucsb.edu/ws/?pid=26262.

p. 136 on white women and affirmative action: Sally Kohn, "Affirmative Action Has Helped White Women More Than Anyone," *Time*, June 17, 2013, http://ideas.time.com/2013/06/17/affirmative-action-has -helped-white-women-more-than-anyone/.

p. 137 "kind of upstanding white citizen[s] . . . the Ku Klux Klan": Michelle Alexander, *The New Jim Crow: Mass Incarceration in the Age of Colorblindness* (New York: New Press, 2010, 2012), 54.

p. 138 "I'm getting mail": Jesse Curtis, "Awakening the Nation: Mississippi Senator John C. Stennis, the White Countermovement, and the Rise of Colorblind Conservatism, 1947–1964" (master's thesis, Kent State University, 2014), 147.

14 "LIKE YOUR WHOLE WORLD DEPENDED ON IT"

p. 141 "They all hate": "Red Neck New York: Is This Wallace Country?," *New York Magazine*, October 7, 1968, 25.

p. 141 "Segregation now": Inaugural address of Governor George Wallace, January 14, 1963, Alabama Department of Archives & History, http://digital.archives.alabama.gov/cdm/ref/collection/voices/id/2952.

p. 142 "into 'our' streets": Dan T. Carter, *From George Wallace to Newt Gingrich: Race in the Conservative Revolution* (Baton Rouge: Louisiana State University Press, 1996), 15.

p. 142 "pace of civil rights": William Brink and Louis Harris, *Black and White: A Study of U.S. Racial Attitudes Today* (New York: Simon and Schuster, 1966), 100, 120.

p. 143 "so forward": Brink and Harris, *Black and White*, 120.

p. 144 "excesses . . . that come to nothing": Kenneth O'Reilly, *Nixon's Piano: Presidents and Racial Politics from Washington to Clinton* (New York: The Free Press, 1996), 281.

p. 145 "THIS TIME VOTE": "The First Civil Right," Nixon campaign ad, 1968, http://www.livingroomcandidate.org/commercials/1968, accessed August 8, 2015.

p. 145 "hits it right on the nose": Carter, *From George Wallace to Newt Gingrich*, 30.

p. 145 "two of the civil rights movement's greatest victories": O'Reilly, *Nixon's Piano*, 296.

15 IN THE CROSSHAIRS: THE VRA

p. 147 "weaken the enforcement": Ari Berman, *Give Us the Ballot: The Modern Struggle for Voting Rights in America* (New York: Farrar, Straus and Giroux, 2015), 74.

p. 148 "resistance to the program . . . perfected": Berman, *Give Us the Ballot*, 76.

p. 149 "aimed at the subtle": *Allen v. State Board of Elections*, 393 US 544 (1969), https://www.oyez.org/cases/1968/3.

p. 149 "350 years of oppression": Berman, *Give Us the Ballot*, 76.

p. 149 "an institution for law enforcement": *Give Us the Ballot*, 77.

p. 150 "just looking for trouble": *ABC News Turning Point*, "Murder in Mississippi: The Price of Freedom," produced by Anthony Ross Potter (New York: ABC News, 1994), VHS.

p. 150 "targeted at those": Department of Justice, "History of Federal Voting Rights Laws: The Voting Rights Act of 1965, the 1965 Enactment," http://www.justice.gov/crt/about/vot/intro/intro_b.php, accessed July 30, 2015.

p. 151 "Congress had found": *South Carolina v. Katzenbach*, 383 US 301, 327–28 (1966).

p. 151 on Nixon's first civil rights legislation: Berman, *Give Us the Ballot*, 77.

p. 152 "With the entire . . . in the nation": Berman, *Give Us the Ballot*, 78.

p. 152 Thurmond and Mitchell exchange: Berman, *Give Us the Ballot*, 83.

16 BEATING DOWN *BROWN* (AGAIN!)

p. 155 "time was too short": *Brown v. Board of Education*, 349 US 294 (1955).

p. 156 "Segregation of . . . our states": Jason Sokol, *All Eyes Are Upon Us: Race and Politics from Boston to Brooklyn* (New York: Basic Books, 2014).

p. 156 "I consider my": Richard Nixon, *RN: The Memoirs of Richard Nixon* (New York: Simon & Schuster, 1978).

p. 158 "makes education a function": *Rodriguez v. San Antonino Independent School District*, 337 F Supp. 280 (1971).

p. 159 "there is no fundamental right": *San Antonio Independent School District v. Rodriguez*, 411 US 1 (1973).

p. 159 Justice Lewis Powell's opinion: *San Antonio Independent School District v. Rodriguez*, 411 US 1 (1973).

p. 162 "these children were kept": Samantha Meinke, *"Milliken v Bradley*: The Northern Battle for Desegregation," *Michigan Bar Journal* (September 2011), 20.

p. 162–63 on ruling in *Milliken v. Bradley*: *Milliken v. Bradley*, 418 US 717 (1974).

p. 165 on ruling in *Bakke*: *Regents of the University of California v. Bakke*, 438 US 265 (1978); Lewis Powell to William Brennan, memo, July 23, 1978, *Bakke* 76–811, Folder 10, Lewis Powell Papers, Washington and Lee School of Law, http://law2.wlu.edu/powellarchives/page.asp?pageid=1322, accessed July 7, 2015.

p. 165 "bore no responsibility": William G. Bowen and Derek Bok, *The Shape of the River: Long-Term Consequences of Considering Race in College and University Admissions* (Princeton, NJ: Princeton University Press, 1998), 8.

p. 165 "I do not accept that position": Justice Byron R. White, Memorandum for the Conference, October 13, 1977, Powell Papers, Washington and Lee School of Law, http://supremecourtopinions.wustl.edu /files/opinion_pdfs/1977/76-811.pdf, accessed April 23, 2018.

p. 165 "the most pervasive and ingenious forms": Justice Marshall dissent, First Printed Draft, June 28, 1978 (2 of 2), *Bakke* 76-811, Powell Papers, Washington and Lee School of Law, http://law2.wlu.edu /powellarchives/page.asp?pageid=1322, accessed July 7, 2015.

17 THE REAGAN REVOLUTION

p. 169 "part Wallace and part Nixon": O'Reilly, *Nixon's Piano*, 355.

p. 170 "racism with plausible deniability": Comment by Hugh Jim Bissell on August 13, 2015, at 07:01:07 AM PDT, https://www.dailykos.com /story/2015/08/11/1411087/-Head-of-Dept-of-History-at-West-Point-destroys -argument-that-Civil-War-wasnt-fought-over-slavery?detail=emailclassic, accessed August 15, 2015.

p. 170 "By 1968, you can't": Bob Herbert, "Impossible, Ridiculous, Repugnant," *New York Times*, October 6, 2005.

p. 171 "a faceless mass": Curtis, "Awakening the Nation," 147.

p. 171 "the needier the student": Mark Green and Gail MacColl, *There He Goes Again: Ronald Reagan's Reign of Error* (New York: Pantheon Books, 1983), 89.

p. 172 "under the impression that the problem": Green and MacColl, *There He Goes Again*, 116.

p. 172 "jump through every hoop": William Bradford Reynolds, "Individualism vs. Group Rights: The Legacy of *Brown*," *Yale Law Journal* 93, no. 6 (May 1984): 1002–3.

p. 173 on school lunches: Jonathan Harsch, "Reagan Cuts Eat into School Lunches," *Christian Science Monitor*, September 17, 1981, http://www.csmonitor.com/1981/0917/091746.html, accessed August 14, 2015.

p. 173 "'urban' program that survived the cuts" Peter Dreier, "Reagan's Legacy: Homelessness in America," National Homelessness Institute, *Shelter Online*, no. 135 (May–June 2004), http://www.nhi.org/online/issues/135/reagan.html, accessed January 12, 2010.

p. 174 "other divisions of Government" Howell Raines, "Reagan Aims to Cut 37,000 Federal Jobs, Saving $1.3 Billion," *New York Times*, March 7, 1981.

p. 175 "civil rights gains . . . in danger" Vermon E. Jordan Jr. and John E. Jacob, "Introduction," *The State of Black America, 1982* (New York: National Urban League, 1982), vii.

p. 175 "in virtually every area of life": David H. Swinton, "Economic Status of Blacks, 1987," *The State of Black America, 1988* (New York: National Urban League, 1988), 136.

p. 176 "failure . . . vast majority of average black Americans": Swinton, "Economic Status of Blacks, 1987," 136.

p. 176 "virtually ensured that the goal": Hanes Walton, *African American Power and Politics* (New York: Columbia University Press, 1997), 26.

18 CRACK

p. 179 Ronald Reagan's radio address: "Radio Address to the Nation on Federal Drug Policy," October 2, 1982, The American Presidency Project, www.ucsb.edu/ws/?pid=43085, accessed July 6, 2015.

p. 181 "Reagan signed a secret order": Michael Schaller, *Ronald Reagan* (New York: Oxford University Press), 75.

p. 181 "moral equivalent of the Founding Fathers": Schaller, *Ronald Reagan*, 40.

p. 184 "I remain convinced": "High Crimes and Misdemeanors: The Iran-Contra Scandal," *Frontline*, November 27, 1990, http://billmoyers.com/content/high-crimes-misdemeanors-reagan-iran-contra-scandal, accessed August, 29, 2015.

p. 185 "led a charmed life:" Alexander Cockburn and Jeffrey St. Clair, *Whiteout: The CIA, Drugs, and the Press* (London: Verso, 1998), 9.

p. 185 "no one has yet demonstrated": Andrew B. Whitford and Jeff Yates, *Presidential Rhetoric and the Public Agenda: Constructing the War on Drugs* (Baltimore: Johns Hopkins University Press, 2009), 97.

p. 186 "Drugs are menacing" Ronald Reagan, "Speech to the Nation on the Campaign Against Drug Abuse," September 14, 1986, http://millercenter.org/president/reagan/speeches/speech-5465, accessed November 16, 2015.

p. 186 "rapidly spreading into the suburbs": Tom Morganthau, Mark Miller, Janet Huck, and Jeanne DeQuinne, "Kids and Cocaine," *Newsweek*, March 17, 1986.

p. 186 "epidemic . . . the wealthiest suburbs": Peter Kerr, "Extra-Potent Cocaine: Use Rising Sharply Among Teen-Agers," *New York Times*, March 20, 1986.

p. 187 "gains made over the past 25 years" Lee P. Brown, "Crime in the Black Community," *The State of Black America, 1988* (New York: National Urban League, 1988), 102.

p. 187 "Between 1984 and 1994, the homicide rate for Black males" Roland G. Fryer Jr., Paul S. Heaton, Steven D. Levitt, and Kevin M. Murphy, "Measuring Crack Cocaine and Its Impact," *Economic Inquiry* 51, no. 3 (July 2013): 1651–52.

p. 188 "represents a break from decades of convergence" Fryer Jr. et al., "Measuring Crack Cocaine and Its Impact," 1651–52.

p. 188 "a person must possess 500 grams of powder cocaine" NAACP, "Bill to End 100:1 Crack/Powder Cocaine Sentencing Disparity Will Soon Go Before the Full House of Representatives," http://www.naacp.org/action-alerts/entry/bill-to-end-100-1-crack-powder-cocaine-sentencing-disparity-will-soon-go/, accessed November 16, 2015.

19 "STREETS CLEARED OF GARBAGE"

p. 193 "TULIA'S STREETS CLEARED OF GARBAGE": Andrew Gumbel, "American Travesty," the *Independent*, August 20, 2002, https://archive.commondreams.org/headlines02/0820-06.htm.

p. 196 "a mass lynching . . . string you up anyway": Gumbel, "American Travesty."

p. 197 Human Rights Watch quote and information: Human Rights Watch, "Incarcerated America," http://www.hrw.org/legacy/backgrounder /usa/incarceration/us042903.pdf, accessed August 17, 2015.

p. 197 University of Washington study: Alexander, *The New Jim Crow*, 126–27.

p. 197 "United States did not face": Naomi Murakawa, *The First Civil Right: How Liberals Built Prison America* (New York: Oxford University Press, 2014), 3.

20 OBAMA

p. 199 "The country" and **"really majestic"** "Reaction to Obama Elected 1st Black US President," *USA Today*, November 5, 2008, http:// usatoday30.usatoday.com/news/world/2008-11-05-1271317715_x.htm, accessed September 1, 2015.

p. 200 "people of color": "Reaction to Obama Elected 1st Black US President," USA Today, November 5, 2008, posted November 5, 2008, http: //usatoday30.usatoday.com/news/world/2008-11-05-1271317715_x.htm, accessed September 1, 2015.

p. 200 "Historic Win" "Obama's Victory on Newspaper Front Pages" slideshows, *Huffington Post*, December 6, 2008, http://www.huffingtonpost .com/2008/11/05/obamas-victory-on-newspap_n_141311.html, accessed September 1, 2015.

p. 200–01 "It's a bad thing . . . Utah?": Andrew O'Hehir, "I Watched Fox News for Five Hours Last Night," *Salon*, November 6, 2008, https://www .salon.com/2008/11/06/watching_fox, accessed September 3, 2015.

p. 201–02 "Conservatives were looking . . . new schemes": Jane Mayer, "The Voter Fraud Myth," *New Yorker*, October 29, 2012.

p. 202 "I don't want everybody . . . goes down": Ari Berman, "The GOP War on Voting: In a Campaign Supported by the Koch Brothers, Republicans Are Working to Prevent Millions of Democrats from Voting Next Year," *Rolling Stone*, August 30, 2011.

p. 202 "model voter-ID legislation": Jim Rutenberg, "This Looks Like a National Strategy: Interview of Ari Berman," *New York Times Magazine*, August 17, 2015.

p. 203 "perpetrating one of the greatest frauds": "ACORN Accusations: McCain Makes Exaggerated Claims of 'Voter Fraud.' Obama

Soft-Pedals His Connections," Factcheck.org, October 18, 2008, http://www
.factcheck.org/2008/10/acorn-accusations, accessed August 28, 2015.

p. 203 "a 52% majority of GOP voters": Katie Connolly, "Poll: Majority
of Republicans Believe ACORN Stole the Presidential Election," *Newsweek*,
November 9, 2009, http://www.newsweek.com/poll-majority-republicans
-believe-acorn-stole-presidential-election-210966, accessed September 5, 2015.

p. 204 "it is an exceedingly dumb strategy": Richard L. Hasen, *The
Voting Wars: From Florida 2000 to the Next Election Meltdown* (New Haven, CT:
Yale University Press, 2012), 61.

p. 204 "You can't steal an election": Mayer, "The Voter Fraud Myth."

p. 205 "only 8% of whites" NAACP and NAACP Legal Defense and
Educational Fund, "Defending Democracy: Confronting Modern Barriers to
Voting Rights in America," 4.

p. 208 "an unreasonable burden": Sari Horwitz, "Pennsylvania Judge
Strikes Down Voter ID Law," *Washington Post*, January 17, 2014, https://www
.washingtonpost.com/world/national-security/pennsylvania-judge-strikes
-downvoter-id-law/2014/01/17/472d620e-7fa2-11e3-93c10e888170b723_story
.html, accessed September 5, 2015.

p. 209 "I know that the cutting": "Former Florida GOP Leaders Say
Voter Suppression Was Reason They Pushed New Election Law," *Palm Beach
Post*, November 25, 2012, https://www.palmbeachpost.com/news/state
-regional-govt-politics/former-florida-gop-leaders-say-voter-suppression-was
-reason-they-pushed-new-election-law/R9iQlcYqCBY3k1u4k5XdLP/,
accessed September 8, 2015.

21 *SHELBY COUNTY V. HOLDER*: GUTTING THE VRA

p. 214 "Congress drew reasonable conclusions": Leadership
Conference on Civil Rights, "*Shelby County v. Holder*," http://www.civilrights
.org/voting-rights/shelby-county-v-holder.html?referrer=https://www.bing
.com, accessed November 18, 2015.

p. 214 "Largely because of the Voting Rights Act": *Shelby County v.
Holder*, 570 U.S.2 (2013).

p. 218 "creates an unconstitutional burden on": *Veasey et al. v. Perry
et al.*, No. 14–41127 (October 14, 2014).

p. 218 "substantially injure": In Re: State of Texas, Petitioner, On
Petition for Writ of Mandamus to the United States District Court for the

Southern District of Texas, Corpus Christi Division Cases No. 2:13-CV-193 (lead case), 2:13-CV-263 and 2:13-CV-291 (consolidated).

p. 218 "This is not a run-of-the-mill case": *Veasey, et al. v. Perry, et al.,* No. 14–41127 (October 14, 2014).

p. 219 Ginsburg's dissent: *Veasey et al. v. Perry et al.*

p. 220 "Texas will continue to fight for its": Erik Eckholm, "Texas ID Law Called Breach of Voting Rights Act," *New York Times,* August 5, 2015, http://www.nytimes.com/2015/08/06/us/appellate-panel-says-texas-id-law-broke-us-voting-rights-act.html, accessed September 6, 2015.

p. 221 "Congress is less popular than": Mollie Reilly, "Congress Approval Rating Drops to Dismal 5 Percent in Poll," *Huffington Post,* October 9, 2013, http://www.huffingtonpost.com/2013/10/09/congress-approval-rating_n_4069899.html, accessed September 7, 2015.

22 "WHY WOULD THEY TRY TO MAKE PEOPLE HATE US?"

p. 223 Obama's disapproval rating among the GOP: "President Obama Job Approval Among Republicans," http://www.realclearpolitics.com/epolls/other/president_obama_job_approval_among_republicans-1047.html, accessed September 7, 2015.

p. 224 candidate Obama's need for Secret Service protection: "Obama Placed Under Secret Service Protection," CNN, May 3, 2007, http://www.cnn.com/2007/POLITICS/05/03/obama.protection/index.html?eref=weather, accessed September 6, 2015.

p. 224 "a sharp and very disturbing increase" and "Why would they try to": Rachel Weiner, "Behind the Scenes: Newsweek on McCain in the Dark, Obama Threats, and More," *Huffington Post,* December 6, 2008, http://www.huffingtonpost.com/2008/11/05/obama-we-cant-solve-globa_n_141358.html, accessed September 6, 2015.

p. 224 "Should Obama be killed?": Earl Ofari Hutchinson, "Facebook Thinks Praying for President Obama's Assassination Is Okay," *Huffington Post,* June 29, 2010, http://www.huffingtonpost.com/earl-ofari-hutchinson/facebook-thinks-praying-f_b_558044.html, accessed September 6, 2015.

p. 225 "this president would learn": Rachel Weiner, "John Sununu, the Worst Surrogate?" *Washington Post,* July 17, 2012, http://www.washingtonpost.com/blogs/the-fix/post/john-sununu-mitt-romneys-bestworst- surrogate/2012/ 07/17/gJQATJXSrW_blog.html, accessed September 6, 2015.

p. 225 "I do not believe": Jon Perr, "The Othering of the President," *Daily Kos*, February 22, 2015, accessed August 15, 2015.

p. 225 "f__g n___r": "New Hampshire police commissioner resigns over Obama N-word Slur," the *Guardian*, May 19, 2014, http://www.theguardian .com/world/2014/may/19/new-hampshire-police-commissioner-quits-obama -slur, accessed September 7, 2015.

p. 225 on North Canton, Ohio, police dispatcher: Amanda Terkel, "Ohio Police Dispatcher Passes Along Racist Image of Air Force One," Think Progress, August 16, 2009, http://thinkprogress.org/politics/2009/08 /16/56320/dispatcher-ohio-pic, September 7, 2015.

p. 225 "Paradox of progress": William Jelani Cobb, *The Substance of Hope: Barack Obama and the Paradox of Progress* (New York: Walker and Co., 2010).

p. 227 "retrograde species": Richard Cohen, "Dylann Roof, the Charleston Murders and Hate in the Mainstream," Southern Poverty Law Center, https://medium.com/@splcenter/dylann-roof-the-charleston-murders -and-hate-in-the-mainstream-4ce1311bb140, accessed July 25, 2015.

p. 228 "$65,000 to Republican": Jon Swaine, "Leader of group cited in 'Dylann Roof manifesto' donated to top Republicans," the *Guardian*, June 22, 2015, https://www.theguardian.com/us-news/2015/jun/21/dylann-roof -manifesto-charleston-shootings-republicans, accessed June 29, 2018.

p. 228 "so nice" and "You're taking over": Sari Horwitz, Chico Harlan, Peter Holley, and William Wan, "What We Know So Far about Charleston Church Shooting Suspect Dylann Roof," *Washington Post*, https:// www.washingtonpost.com/news/post-nation/wp/2015/06/20/what-we-know -so-far-about-charleston-church-shooting-suspect-dylann-roof/ ?noredirect=on&utm_term=.3ca74d61f1d8, accessed April 24, 2018.

EPILOGUE

p. 229 "Don't worry": Fox News Insider, "Trump: 'We're Going to Take the Country Back,'" http://insider.foxnews.com/2015/07/12/donald-trump -phoenix-speech-were-going-take-country-back, accessed September 9, 2015.

PHOTOGRAPH CREDITS

Courtesy of the Library of Congress: xviii, 4, 14, 22, 48,154, 168; Gordon Coster/The LIFE Picture Collection/Getty Images: 58; Alfred R. Waud, courtesy of the Library of Congress: 30; Theodore R. Davis, courtesy of the Art and Picture Collection, The New York Public Library: 40 (top and bottom); Courtesy of the Burton Historical Collection, Detroit Public Library: 72; Hank Walker/The LIFE Picture Collection/Getty Images: 88; Bettmann/Getty Images: 102, 146, 178; Universal Images Group/ Getty Images: 114; Archive Photos/Getty Images: 128; Ted Streshinsky/ Corbis Historical/Getty Images: 140; Joe Raedle/Hulton Archive/Getty Images: 192; Charles Ommanney/Getty Images News/Getty Images: 198; Dave Martin/Associated Press: 212; Win McNamee/Getty Images News/ Getty Images: 222.

INDEX

Note: *Italic* page numbers indicate illustrations.